*m*BIT Coaching Workbook

*"Aligning your head, heart and gut intelligences
to ev*

Over the last decade, the field of Ne_____ _ve complex, adaptive and functional neural networks in both our heart and gut. Called the cardiac and enteric brains respectively, scientific evidence is emerging that these brains exhibit deep intelligence and wisdom.

Now scientific knowledge is finally catching up with profound insights from esoteric and spiritual traditions informing us for thousands of years about these three powerful intelligences. Using leading edge methodologies from the new field of *m*BIT (multiple Brain Integration Techniques) this Coaching Workbook provides a powerful system for supporting, communicating with and integrating the wisdom and intelligence of your multiple brains.

Using the exercises in this *m*BIT Coaching Workbook, and working in close collaboration with the guidance of your *m*BIT Coach, you can deeply amplify your personal evolution and begin to achieve even greater success and happiness in a world of massive change. With this *m*BIT Coaching Workbook you can truly evolve your multiple brains and your world!

*m*BIT Coaching Workbook

GRANT SOOSALU AND MARVIN OKA

www.mbraining.com

First Published 2014
TimeBinding Publications

Contents

*m*BIT Coaching Workbook

*m*BIT Coaching Workbook

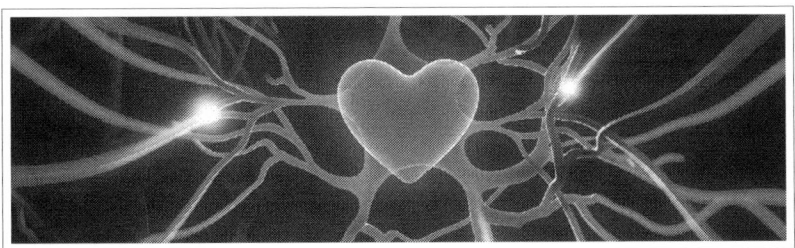

Introduction

"You have to master not only the art of listening to your head, you must also master listening to your heart and listening to your gut."

Carly Fiorina

As shown by numerous converging avenues of neuroscientific and behavioral modeling evidence, and described in detail in our book '*mBraining*', the *m*BIT model says that wisdom is generated through listening to and engaging the innate, intuitive intelligence of all your multiple brains (Heart, Head and Gut) via their Highest Expressions (Compassion, Creativity and Courage). The process for this is to:

1. Engage your neural networks or brains and communicate with them through conscious control of the autonomic gateways (for example by diaphragmatic breathing). Then enable them to communicate with each other.

2. Align your neural networks so you are congruent in your being and your responses.

3. Evolve your self/neural networks in order to function from higher levels of consciousness and the Highest Expressions of your authentic self.

4. Apply this higher level of consciousness and authentic self to practical life situations and thus have greater wisdom in your decisions and actions.

The key to this process is step 4 — in the application of multiple perspectives and Highest Expressions to pragmatic real-world situations. As the noted systems theorist, neuro-biologist and philosopher, Dr. Humberto Maturana highlights, "*All knowing is doing*." You only truly know something when you can use it with deep wisdom and insight to create real-world actions and results.

Wisdom in action

So as indicated, wisdom involves action and expression into the world. Wisdom that is not embodied in pragmatic action is not wisdom at all, it's merely entertaining ideas. Because wisdom only becomes true wisdom when it's pragmatically and consistently applied to practical life situations, this Workbook is designed to facilitate deep explorations into how you are *mBraining* your world — to how you are using your multiple brains in real world situations, in the patterns and behaviors you are using to create your world — and to highlight specific areas of application of the *m*BIT model, roadmap and principles to real world contexts. In conjunction with your *m*BIT Coach, this Workbook can truly assist you to deepen your wisdom and bring more integrated joy, happiness and success to evolve your world!

*m*BIT Coaching Workbook Exercises

This Coaching Workbook contains the following exercise sections for you to explore:

1. Autonomic Mode Patterns – Sympathetic vs Parasympathetic Mode

2. ANS Response Patterns – Fight versus Flight versus Freeze versus Fold versus Tend and Befriend Patterns

3. Neural Syntax Patterns and Preferences

4. Neural Integration Constraint (NIC) Patterns and Preferences

5. Communication Process Exploration

6. Prime Functions Patterns and Preferences

7. Core Competencies Patterns and Preferences

8. Congruence and Alignment Patterns

9. Highest Expressions Exploration

10. Highest Expression Integration

11. Trust Patterns Exploration

12. Neural Integration Blocks (NIB's) Patterns and Preferences

13. Cognitive Dissonance Patterns

14. *m*BIT Toolkit Category Patterns

15. *mBraining* Discovery Exercises

16. Wisdom, Emergence and Personal Evolution

How to do the exercises

1. Do the exercises when you are not rushed, when you have time, space and a conducive environment to explore the questions and deeply involve yourself in the enquiries. Try not to do them just from your *'head'*, but also involve your heart and your gut. Meditate on them, chew over them, dwell on them in your heart. Explore them deeply.

2. Do the exercises firstly in your *'normal'* state and then redo them from an aligned and balanced state. Take a couple of minutes to do Balanced Breathing using the Highest Expressions and the *m*BIT Foundational Sequence. (Your *m*BIT Coach will teach and guide you through this experience.) Do the questions again and note what changes you find. Do you get different or additional insights and distinctions when in a balanced mode?

3. There are no wrong or right answers with these exercises. They're designed to be journeys of exploration into how you are *'mBraining'* your life – how you are using your multiple brains to create your world and reality. Each of us has patterns and habits – unconscious competencies – that our neural networks, as patterning systems, perform for us. In order to evolve your world, you need to first become aware of your existing patterns, then you need to explore these patterns, the outcomes they create and the underlying values and secondary gains that support them, and then you need to align and integrate around them, to evolve your intentions, actions and consequences and ultimately your brains and the very neural networks that bring forth you and your world.

4. After you have finished an Exercise, take a moment to fill in the *'Generative Learning: Future Pacing the next mBIT Coaching Session'* section at the end of the exercise. This is designed to help you generalize your learnings, open up your unconscious and conscious minds to new possibilities, encourage you to ask yourself *'what else?, where else?, what if?'*, and to future pace your insights and learnings into the next coaching session and thereby make the most of your work and time with your *m*BIT Coach.

5. Most importantly, have fun with exploring these exercises. Bring a sense of creativity and playfulness to how you approach them. The design of the exercises is to first bring awareness to your inner and outer worlds and your patterns and unconscious competencies. Next they help you uncover skill gaps and opportunities for growth and personal evolution. Finally, they engender experiences of possibility, hope and a sense of a higher expression of self, that working together with your *m*BIT Coach you can more deeply explore and bring to life at your next Coaching session. And of course, with your innate intuitive intelligence at play, you can be delightfully surprised at what emerges and evolves in your world.

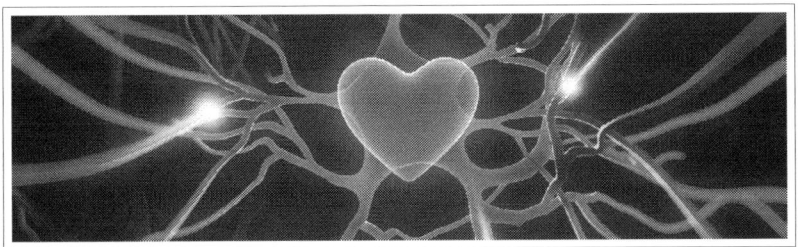

1.

Autonomic Mode

In order to work effectively and gain skills with your multiple brains and their functions and competencies, it helps to understand the role of your Autonomic Nervous System (ANS) and how it affects the quality of the way your brains operate.

Your nervous system has two major divisions, the voluntary and the autonomic. The Voluntary System is mainly concerned with movement and sensation. The Autonomic Nervous System on the other hand is responsible for control of involuntary and visceral bodily functions. The functions it controls include:

- Cardiovascular
- Respiratory
- Digestive
- Urinary
- Reproductive functions
- The body's response to stress

It's called *'autonomic'* because it operates largely automatically and outside of conscious control. It's divided into two separate branches — the sympathetic and parasympathetic. These two branches work in a delicately tuned, reciprocal and (usually) opposing fashion. Simplistically, the sympathetic system can be considered to be the '*fight or flight*' system. It allows the body to function under stress and danger. The parasympathetic system is the '*feeding and fornicating*' arm. It controls the vegetative functions of feeding, breeding, rest and repose. The parasympathetic system also provides constant opposition to the sympathetic system to bring your total system into balance or homeostasis.

In times of danger or stress, the sympathetic system, which has a very fast onset and response, kicks in and gets you moving to handle or resolve the situation. The slower acting parasympathetic system begins to operate after the danger has passed, and brings you back to normalcy. Without the opposing function of the parasympathetic system your body would stay amped up, burning energy and fuel and eventually exhaust itself.

Why is this important?

The reason you want to know about the sympathetic and parasympathetic systems is because they innervate and impact the heart, gut and head brains. There are major connections between the head brain hemispheres, the cardiac brain, the enteric brain and these sympathetic and parasympathetic arms of the ANS. And as the two ANS components work in opposing ways, the dominance of one or the other leads to very different modes of processing throughout our multiple brains. In this way the '*Autonomic Mode*' strongly influences how the multiple brains operate.

For example, in the gut, parasympathetic activity enhances intestinal peristaltic movement promoting nourishment during quiescence, whereas sympathetic activity inhibits such activity during times when physical exertion requires catabolic (energy) mobilization. Parasympathetic activity generally slows the heart, whereas sympathetic activity accelerates it.

You'll notice here that a powerful functional principle of opponent processing is operating for autonomic control across your total system. Your brains can function in ways that are sympathetic dominant, parasympathetic dominant, or some combination of the two, and each of these systems typically opposes the other. You can see this opponent processing clearly at work by examining details of what each system activates.

Sympathetic activation

Activation of the sympathetic nervous system has the following effects:

- Dilates the pupils and opens the eyelids
- Stimulates the sweat glands
- Dilates the blood vessels in the large skeletal muscles
- Constricts the blood vessels in the rest of the body
- Increases heart rate
- Relaxes and opens up the bronchial tubes of the lungs
- Contracts the sphincter of the bladder and the bladder wall relaxes
- Shuts down and inhibits the secretions in the digestive system
- Can lead to involuntary defecation
- Is associated with Right Hemisphere activation and dominance in the head brain

Parasympathetic activation

Activation of the parasympathetic nervous system has the following effects:

- Constricts the pupils
- Activates and increases the secretion of the salivary glands
- Stimulates the secretions of the stomach
- Decreases heart rate
- Constricts the bronchial tubes and stimulates secretions in the lungs
- Stimulates the activity of the gastro intestinal tract
- Is involved in sexual arousal
- Is associated with Left Hemisphere activation and dominance in the head brain

In this section of the Workbook, you will explore your patterns of Autonomic mode and sympathetic or parasympathetic response and dominance. We each have differing patterns, habits and preferences for orienting to stress and to the world. Some people have tendencies to always operate from a sympathetic or stress dominance. Others tend to be down-regulated and operating largely from states of parasympathetic dominance. Or you might flip between these in various ways and amounts. Each of us is different, and can respond differently in a variety of contexts and situations. Knowing about your typical patterns and preferences, your '*unconscious competencies*' can increase your self-awareness and allow you to begin gaining more choice, control and wisdom in how you are driving and using your multiple brains.

Exploring Your Autonomic Mode Patterns

 Do you have any overall patterns of Autonomic Nervous System (ANS) mode in your life? For example, are you chronically stressed, hyper-vigilant or in high energy mode (sympathetic dominant mode)? Or are you typically tired, depressed, suffer from malaise or in low energy, recuperation mode (parasympathetic dominant mode)? Or do you flip between these states?

Are there triggers, contexts, people or situations that put you into sympathetic dominant (stressed) mode?

Are there triggers, contexts, people or situations that put you into parasympathetic dominant (low energy, depressed) mode?

What strategies do you typically use to shift yourself from overly sympathetic dominant (stressed) mode?

? What strategies do you typically use to shift yourself from overly parasympathetic dominant (depressed) mode?

Are you able to notice or calibrate what mode you are in during your day? Do you have good awareness levels about your state and whether you are overly stressed or depressed? Are you easily able to track your stress and energy levels? What strategies do you use to track your state and to notice *'how'* you are creating your own responses and *'reality'*?

Are you able to notice and calibrate what your breathing is doing during your day? Do you have good awareness of your breathing patterns, both the timing and duration of your in-breaths and out-breaths, as well as which part of your lungs you are breathing from (high in the chest, middle of the chest, diaphragm etc.)? How can you bring even more attention to this? What impacts will this have on your life?

What are the activities, things, people or experiences that make you feel revitalized, calm, refreshed and renewed? How can you plan for and make time for more of these in your life? What will a more balanced, renewed and vital you feel like? What difference will this make in your life?

Generative Learning: Future Pacing the next *m*BIT Coaching Session

Reflections and Learnings

Points to discuss at the next session

Coaching outcomes I'd like to pursue/explore

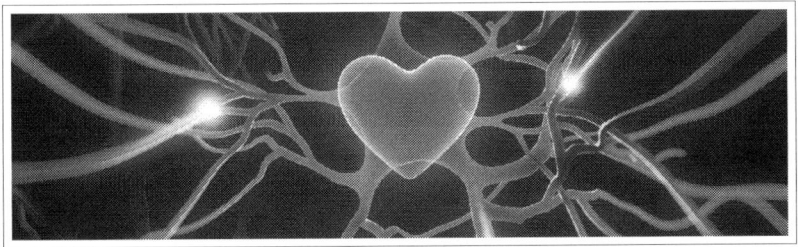

2.

ANS Response Patterns

As explored in the previous exercise, each person has both learned and habitual patterns of Autonomic Nervous System (ANS) activation, also called your Autonomic mode. People can be in various patterns of sympathetic over-dominance (overly stressed or up-regulated), parasympathetic over-dominance (overly depressed or down-regulated), in a nicely balanced mode between the two, or bouncing between the two with both operating at the same time. The sympathetic mode is known simplistically as the '*Fight or Flight*' mode. And the parasympathetic mode is often simplistically referred to as the '*Rest and Repose*' mode, or the '*Feeding and Fornicating*' mode, since it gets evoked during feeding and sexuality.

However, there is much more complexity in how you respond when in these various modes. There is a huge difference between fighting and flighting, and between resting, eating and fornicating or connecting deeply with others. Some people have habits and patterns of fighting and getting aggressive when stressed. Others tend to want to withdraw and do flighting or running away from the situation. Still others can rebound from stress, straight into a deep parasympathetic '*Freeze*' response, or else into such parasympathetic responses as those of '*Folding*' or '*Tending and Befriending*'.

It is incredibly useful to understand your patterns of ANS response to stressors. With awareness you begin to open up choice. The more you know about your patterns and your habitual unconscious responses and triggers, the greater the wisdom and freedom you can bring to your life. The following exercises will help you explore your ANS response patterns and provide useful information for you and your *m*BIT Coach to work with.

Exploring Your ANS Response Patterns

 Do you have any overall or repeated patterns of Autonomic Nervous System (ANS) response in your life? For example, in stressful, threatening or challenging situations do you typically 'Fight' (e.g. become angry and defensive), or 'Flight' (e.g. withdraw or run away), or do you usually 'Freeze' (e.g. shutdown), or perhaps 'Fold' (e.g. capitulate and give in), or do you prefer to 'Tend and Befriend' (e.g. focus on bonding with other people and maintaining relationships with them)?

In what contexts, situations or degrees of stress would you typically:

Fight?

Flight?

Freeze?

Fold/Capitulate?

Tend and Befriend?

Are there contexts, people or situations in which your responses listed above do not serve you wisely or you could handle more generatively and wisely? How does this impact your life and your sense of self?

Generative Learning: Future Pacing the next *m*BIT Coaching Session

Reflections and Learnings

Points to discuss at the next session

Coaching outcomes I'd like to pursue/explore

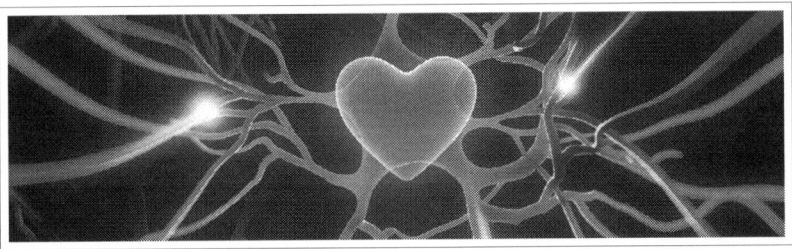

3.

Neural Syntax (Brain) Patterns

As a generalization, people have patterns or preferences in how they filter the world, how they utilize their neural networks or *'brains'* and how they integrate or process their experience through their head, heart and gut brains.

We all know someone who is *'all heart'*, the person who always leads with their heart-based emotions, who focuses primarily (either positively or negatively) on connecting with others, or on dreams, values and their heart's-desires. We say that people like this are *'people people'* and they often *'wear their hearts on their sleeves'*. Their lives, decisions and actions are always heartfelt.

On the other hand, I'm sure you know someone who is *'super-logical'*, who lives through logic, through always over-thinking, through language and through their head brain. Such people are often very dissociated from their emotions, from their heart, and can also be disconnected from their gut-based intuitions. If it isn't logical, then they just won't do it.

Then there's the gutsy people, the ones predominantly connected with their visceral feelings of intuition and courage. They take action and think about it later. They're gung-ho. Logic isn't their strong point, and often neither are the sensitive emotions of love and compassion. They are the action heroes. No fear. Their motto is '*no pain, no gain!'*

While the above descriptions are characterizations, and very few people fit those descriptions in all contexts of life, they nevertheless resound because we've all met people who fit the moulds we've just described. But most people are a bit more well-rounded than that. And the reason is that while people have a pattern or preference for which brain they tend to use as the primary neural network to process, filter and respond to life, we all tend to then have a secondary and tertiary preference for which brain next adds into the process.

In the field of *m*BIT this sequence of brain use is called the neural syntax. This is the sequence, or '*syntax*', by which we construct our experience and reality. We make meaning and sense of our world by using our various brains to process our experience. For some people this pattern involves typically processing with the heart first, then the head and then the gut. For others it might be head then gut, and the heart doesn't even get a look-in. We are all different, and our patterns can also be contextual. But we definitely all have our habitual patterns and preferences. And how you use your brains, the sequence of how they communicate and integrate together, makes a massive difference to the results you create.

So in this exercise you'll explore your preferred patterns of brain use and neural syntax. You can do this for a particular context, or as an overall pattern in your life. Your preference for the sequence in which you use your brains provides you with strengths and weaknesses, so it's quite powerful and instructive to uncover your habitual patterns and preferences for this.

Brain Preferences

On a scale of 0 to 5, where 0 is no skill (or no perceived use or preference) whatsoever, and 5 represents the most skill you can imagine (or most perceived use or preference), rate yourself in how much facility you have with each of your brains (head, heart, gut).

Head (place a circle or X below to rate your level of skill and competence)

(No Skill) **0** - - - - - **1** - - - - - **2** - - - - - **3** - - - - - **4** - - - - - **5** (Magnificent Skill)
(or preference)   (or preference)

Heart (place a circle or X below to rate your level of skill and competence)

(No Skill) **0** - - - - - **1** - - - - - **2** - - - - - **3** - - - - - **4** - - - - - **5** (Magnificent Skill)
(or preference)   (or preference)

Gut (place a circle or X below to rate your level of skill and competence)

(No Skill) **0** - - - - - **1** - - - - - **2** - - - - - **3** - - - - - **4** - - - - - **5** (Magnificent Skill)
(or preference)   (or preference)

Sequence: Do you have a preferred sequence in which you use your brains e.g. do you prefer to use your heart first and then your head, or your head first and then your gut etc.? (You might find it useful in answering this question to remember and revisit some specific instances in which you have recently made a decision.)

Contexts: Are there specific contexts or situations in which you prefer to use one brain over another or one sequence over another? How does this impact your life? What benefits or disadvantages does it bring you?

Generative Learning: Future Pacing the next *m*BIT Coaching Session

Reflections and Learnings

Points to discuss at the next session

Coaching outcomes I'd like to pursue/explore

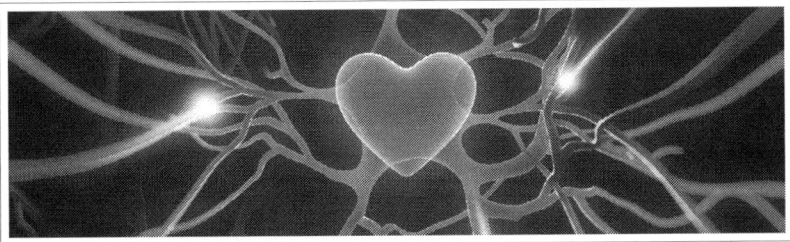

4.

Neural Integration Constraint Patterns

Behavioral modeling research in the field of *m*BIT has uncovered that there are five major classes of issues that arise for people when their brains are not aligned or integrated fully. These are known as *m*BIT Integration Constraints and are ways in which you may inappropriately utilize your head, heart and gut intelligences so that you create problems in achieving the success and happiness you desire in life.

Processes that limit or constrain multiple brain integration:

1. When one intelligence is used to the exclusion of the others

2. When one intelligence swamps or overrides the others

3. When one intelligence is used inappropriately to do the job or prime function of the others

4. When one or more of the three intelligences are in conflict or antagonism with each other

5. When the intelligences are working together but are used in the *'wrong'* sequence for achieving the outcome

Probably one of the easiest ways to determine if you suffer from one or more of the above constraints is if you see evidence in your life of non-alignment of your brains. Look through the following list to see if any relate to you.

*m*BIT Non-Alignment Indicators

The clues that will alert you when your brains are not aligned or integrated:

- You experience internal conflict between your thoughts, feelings and actions
- You've not acted upon your dreams, goals and plans
- You do unwanted behaviors or habits and don't know why or have difficulty in stopping
- You find it difficult to make a decision(s)
- Something within you is making it difficult for you to motivate yourself to take action
- You sabotage yourself from achieving your goals

Exploring your Neural Integration Patterns

 Are there specific times, contexts or situations in which you experience internal conflict between your thoughts, feelings and actions? How specifically does this play out? Are there any patterns with this? And how does this impact your life?

Are there specific times, contexts or situations in which you have not acted upon your dreams, goals and plans? What are the details of this and what are the patterns you see in your life with this? How does this impact your life?

Are there specific times, contexts or situations in which you do unwanted behaviors or habits and don't know why or have difficulty in stopping? How specifically does this play out? And how does this impact your life?

Are there specific times, contexts or situations in which you find it difficult to make a decision(s)? How specifically does this play out? What are the patterns in this? How does this impact your life?

Are there specific times, contexts or situations in which something within you makes it difficult for you to motivate yourself to take action? How specifically does this play out? And how does this impact your life?

Are there specific times, contexts or situations in which you sabotage yourself from achieving your goals? How specifically do you do this? Are there any patterns in this? How does this impact your life?

Are there specific times, contexts or situations in which one of your intelligences or brains is used to the exclusion of the others? What are the details of this? What are the patterns? And how does this impact your life?

Are there specific times, contexts or situations in which one of your intelligences or brains swamps or overrides the others? What are the details of this? What are the patterns? And how does this impact your life?

Are there specific times, contexts or situations in which one of your intelligences or brains is used inappropriately to do the job or Prime Function of the others? What are the details of this? What are the patterns? And how does this impact your life?

Are there specific times, contexts or situations in which one or more of your intelligences or brains are in conflict or antagonism with each other? What are the details of this? What are the patterns? And how does this impact your life?

Are there specific times, contexts or situations in your intelligences or brains are working together but are used in the wrong sequence? What are the details of this? What are the patterns? And how does this impact your life?

Generative Learning: Future Pacing the next *m*BIT Coaching Session

Reflections and Learnings

Points to discuss at the next session

Coaching outcomes I'd like to pursue/explore

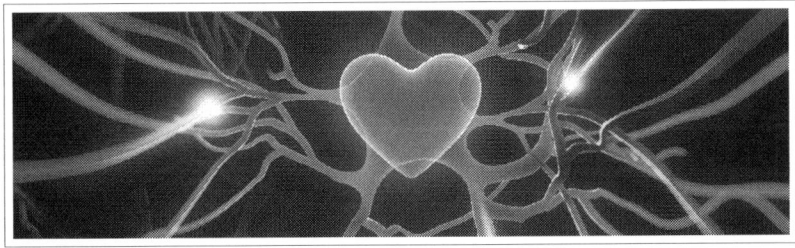

5.

Neural Communication Patterns

Communication is all about listening to the feedback from *and* between the brains, and is a required component for building trust. If one brain refuses to communicate with another or stonewalls and ignores the communication it's receiving, this quickly destroys trust. Communication is about listening and sharing. Always listen with respect to every message that comes from each of your multiple brains and acknowledge them. The messages are important and provide valuable information you disregard at your peril. As a wise person once told us, "*the facts are our friends.*"

From an *mBraining* perspective, it helps to remember that each neural network communicates its unique form of '*facts*' based on its prime functions and particular mode of communication. It's important that each brain works harmoniously with each other's '*facts*' and you are sensitive to each brain's unique language and method of communication.

The following lists indicate some of the ways in which the brains communicate and which you can use to begin to become aware of your own patterns and preferences for brain communication and signaling.

The Head communicates via:

☺ Internal dialogue

☺ Internal sounds

☺ Internal images

☺ Internal Kinesthesia (feelings)

☺ Dreams, symbols, visions, words, narratives, metaphor

The Heart communicates via:

♥ Emotions and feelings

♥ Interest, attention and salience

♥ Symbolic images, dreams and visions

♥ Kinesthetic sensations e.g. pain, tightness, warmth etc.

♥ Beats, rhythm

♥ Speed, timing of movements

♥ Breathing

♥ Tones (music, song)

♥ Quiet/small voice and simple words

♥ Heart-based language

♥ Smells

♥ Heart-related health issues

♥ *'Felt-sense'* and body/chest sensations

♥ Electrical signals

The Gut communicates via:

- Hungers, lusts, cravings for foods and satiety signals

- Motivation signals and visceral feelings of attraction, compulsion and repulsion

- Fear signals and visceral feelings of safety and threat e.g. fear, apprehension, foreboding, nagging, etc.

- Peristalsis — swallowing, choking, burping, vomiting, flatulence, excreting

- Kinesthetic/gut visceral sensations e.g. anxiety, butterflies in the stomach, cramping, gut rumblings, unsettled stomach, heartburn, etc.

- Physical movement (including physical hesitation)

- Gut/GIT health issues, immune system issues

- Diaphragmatic breathing

- Belly laughing

- Guttural sounds & simple words

- Quiet/small voice and simple words

- Gut-based language

- Tastes/smells

- Moral disgust and physical disgust, distaste and stench/dis-smell

- *'Felt-sense'* and body/torso sensations

- Dreams/visions

The brains also communicate via *'Gateways'*, these are points of co-innervation (shared nerve connections) between the brains and points that you have both conscious control over as well as autonomic and unconscious connections to. By tracking for signals and feelings in these areas you can often determine when the brains are communicating to you via these gateways. For example, a common experience is to have a *'lump in the throat'* or a feeling of stuckness in the throat area. People say things like, *"I just can't swallow that idea"*, *"This issue sticks in my throat"*, *"It bought a lump to my throat"* – these are all neuro-linguistic indicators of communication from the gut brain to the head brain. The gut brain is tracking for threat and is expressing a message that the issue is not something it can digest or swallow. Since the whole of the esophagus is co-innervated by both the gut brain and the head brain, the gut can control the motor and sensory nerves in the throat and clearly communicate to the head (and to your conscious mind) that it has something to say about the issue.

mBraining Communication Gateways

The bridges or gateways through which conscious communication and control can occur:

1. The face

2. The tongue and throat

3. The hands

4. The diaphragm and intercostals

5. The pelvic floor

6. The feet

In the following exercises you'll explore how your brains communicate with you. Research shows that the more attuned and aware you are of the messages and communication signals from your heart and gut brains, the greater the level of intuitions and inner wisdom you'll be able to bring to your decisions and your life.

Exploring your Neural Communication Patterns

 Take a moment, somewhere quiet, settle and start doing Balanced Breathing (6 seconds in, 6 seconds out). Once you are in balance, talk to your heart, ask it a question. Then begin to notice in what ways your heart intelligence communicates to you. What do you notice? Looking at the list on the previous page, can you get a sense of the communication processes that your heart is using to answer you? Do you hear a voice and words? If so, is it the same or different to the normal voice in your head? Do you hear sounds? Do you see colors, symbols or images? Do feel certain *'felt-sense'* sensations in your chest or body? What do you notice and experience?

Now still doing Balanced Breathing (6 seconds in, 6 seconds out), talk to your gut brain, ask it a question. Begin to notice in what ways your gut intelligence communicates to you. What do you notice? Looking at the list on the previous pages, can you get a sense of the communication processes that your gut is using to answer you? Do you hear a voice and words? If so, is it the same or different to the normal voice in your head? Do you hear sounds? Do you see colors, symbols or images? Do feel certain '*felt-sense*' sensations in your torso or body? Is there gurgling, movements, feelings in your gut or up in your throat? Do you get a sense of taste in your mouth? What do you notice and experience?

Now talk to your head, ask it a question and begin to notice in what ways your head communicates to you. What do you notice? Looking at the list on the previous pages, can you get a sense of the communication processes your head is using to answer you? Do you hear a voice and words? If so, is it the same or different to the normal voice in your head? Do you hear sounds? Do you see colors, symbols or images? Do feel certain '*felt-sense*' sensations in your head or body? What do you notice and experience?

Generative Learning: Future Pacing the next *m*BIT Coaching Session

Reflections and Learnings

Points to discuss at the next session

Coaching outcomes I'd like to pursue/explore

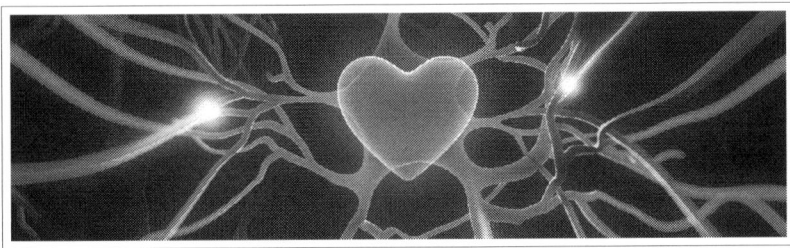

6.

*m*BIT Prime Functions

Your different brains have clearly distinct intelligences, prime functions and underlying core competencies. Each brain is optimized to perform very different functions. In the book *'mBraining'* we describe these in detail, but here we'll just summarize them.

The heart brain...

The heart is the seat of love and desires, goals, dreams and values. When you are connected to something you feel it and value it in your heart. When you hear that someone *'wears their heart on their sleeve'* you intuitively know that this does NOT mean that they are too logical. Instead, this is saying that they show their emotions, desires and intentions too obviously and readily.

If you say something is heartfelt, you aren't saying it's intellectually concise. And when you look at the language patterns of the heart, they express notions of love, connection, kindness and their converse. The prime functions of the heart intelligence involve salience, affection and relational issues such as a deep sense of truth and moral rightness as compared to rule based ethics.

HEART BRAIN PRIME FUNCTIONS

- **EMOTING** – emotional processing (e.g. anger, grief, hatred, joy, happiness etc.)
- **VALUES** – processing what's important to you and your priorities (and its relationship to the emotional strength of your aspirations, dreams, desires, etc.)
- **RELATIONAL AFFECT** – your felt connection with others (e.g. feelings of love/hate/indifference, compassion/uncaring, like/dislike, etc.)

The gut brain...

Due to its evolutionary history, the gut brain is responsible at a core level for determining what will be assimilated into self and excreted from self. It must determine what is required to maintain health and wellness in the system and decide whether molecules ingested into the stomach will be absorbed or excreted. Indeed, research has shown that more than 70 to 80 percent of our immune cells are located in the gut, and the enteric brain is intimately involved in managing immune function.

The prime functions of the gut are around protection, self-preservation, core identity and motility. Back when evolution was at the stage of complexity of sea cucumbers and worms, organisms only had a neural processing system of an enteric brain. This intelligence was used to detect threats and food in the environment and move away from danger and towards food. The gut brain maintains boundary detection and mobilization. In humans it is expressed as motivation, gutsy courage and a gut-felt desire to take action (or not).

GUT BRAIN PRIME FUNCTIONS

- **CORE IDENTITY** – a deep and visceral sense of core-self, and determining at the deepest levels what is '*self*' versus '*not-self*'
- **SELF-PRESERVATION** – protection of self, safety, boundaries, hungers and aversions
- **MOBILIZATION** – motility, impulse for action, gutsy courage and the will to act

The head brain...

In many ways the prime functions of the head brain are obvious, they involve the mental cognitive functions of logical thinking and include the processes of reasoning, perception and how we make meaning. Thought processes involve mental imagery, language expression, abstraction and symbol manipulation. The main job of the head is to intellectually make sense of the world and to provide executive control.

HEAD BRAIN PRIME FUNCTIONS

- **COGNITIVE PERCEPTION** – cognition, perception, pattern recognition, etc.
- **THINKING** – reasoning, abstraction, analysis, synthesis, meta-cognition etc.
- **MAKING MEANING** – semantic processing, languaging, narrative, metaphor, etc.

Exploring Your Heart Brain Prime Functions

 Emoting: Are there any heart-based emotions that challenge you or that you have blocks or difficulties with? For example, emotions you either can't feel or lack in your life? Or ones that take over and you don't have as much control with that you'd like to? Are there any specific contexts or situations that relate to these?

Relational Affect: Do you have any blocks, challenges or difficulties with connecting with others, or building bonds of affection, friendship or deep loving? Do you have any issues with trust? Are there people or contexts that impact your ability to connect with and relate to others?

Values: Do you know what's important to you? Do you have a clear set of values? Do you have dreams and goals that make your heart sing? If not, how are you stopping or limiting yourself?

Generative Learning: Future Pacing the next *m*BIT Coaching Session

Reflections and Learnings

Points to discuss at the next session

Coaching outcomes I'd like to pursue/explore

Exploring Your Gut Brain Prime Functions

 Mobilization: Do you have any blocks, challenges or difficulties in getting moving and taking action in any contexts of your life? Are there areas of life in which you are not easily able to motivate and mobilize yourself? Are there specific times and contexts in which you find yourself procrastinating or stalling? How could you generate more action, movement and motivation in your life?

Self-Preservation: Are there any areas or contexts of life that you experience threat, fear or overwhelm in? What are the triggers? How does this impact your life? How could you feel more secure, more alive and more centered?

Core Identity: Are there any areas or contexts of life in which you don't deeply feel you truly embody your self and who you are? Are there behaviors, thoughts or feelings that you do that don't match who you are deep down and you'd like to change? Are there behaviors, thoughts and feelings that you don't do that you wish you would and that are more aligned with your core-self? Is there some aspect of your core-self that you'd like to improve, that you'd like to make even more awesome? Is there some part of you that you'd like to accept more fully? What would be a sense of self that would truly inspire you deeply?

Generative Learning: Future Pacing the next *m*BIT Coaching Session

Reflections and Learnings

Points to discuss at the next session

Coaching outcomes I'd like to pursue/explore

Exploring Your Head Brain Prime Functions

 Cognitive Perception: Are there any patterns of perceiving that don't serve you? Ways of looking at the world or ways of directing your attention that limit your happiness, peace and success?

Thinking: Do you have, or do, any patterns or habitual ways of thinking that don't serve you? Are you troubled by recurring thoughts that disturb you or lead to unresourceful states? Are there ways of thinking that you could improve or upgrade?

Making Meaning: Are there any stories in your life that aren't serving you well? What are they? Do you have any patterns in your life where you make meaning from your experience in a way that upsets you or is dysfunctional? Are there patterns, beliefs and stories that you could improve and upgrade?

Generative Learning: Future Pacing the next *m*BIT Coaching Session

Reflections and Learnings

Points to discuss at the next session

Coaching outcomes I'd like to pursue/explore

Exploring the Prime Function Constraints

Sometimes people use one Prime Function to do the job of another. One example we've seen was an Entertainer who used valuing of others attention in place of connecting with others. This person didn't like connecting deeply with others and didn't exercise that Prime Function, but instead used values to drive their relationship with others by performing on stage because they wanted to be adored and valued by others as a way of connecting and relating.

 Are there any areas of your life where you use one Prime Function to do the job of another? As you look through the Prime Function list of the three brains, is there one that you might be satisfying by using one of the others in its place? If so, what are the challenges and issues that arise as a result of this? How does this impact your life?

Heart Brain Prime Functions
- Emoting
- Relational Affect
- Values

Gut Brain Prime Functions
- Mobilization
- Self-Preservation
- Core Identity

Head Brain Prime Functions
- Cognitive Perception
- Thinking
- Making Meaning

Generative Learning: Future Pacing the next *m*BIT Coaching Session

Reflections and Learnings

Points to discuss at the next session

Coaching outcomes I'd like to pursue/explore

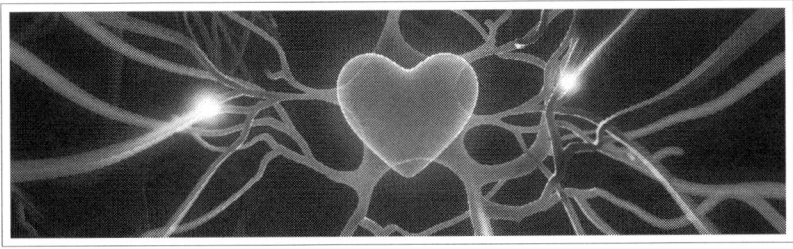

7.

Core Competencies Exploration

Each of your brains (head, heart, gut) has its own domains of expertise and core competencies that it's involved in. In *m*BIT, we have laid these competencies out in a framework that divides the competencies between the brains and across Autonomic mode. You see, the Autonomic Nervous System (ANS) innervates and influences the states and competencies that each of the brains can operate from. When you are stressed and your ANS is sympathetic dominant, you do not feel calm, you can't think clearly and your gut is often in a knot. Similarly, if you are overly depressed and in parasympathetic dominant mode, then your brains cannot function optimally either. You won't be able to think properly, your heart will be down-regulated and your gut will lack vigor and motivation.

The *m*BIT Core Competencies Framework enables you to quickly determine how each of your intelligences is functioning in relation to an issue, and what specific coherent-balanced state might be needed to function optimally and adaptively. Understanding the core competencies helps you quickly recognize how each brain is fulfilling its Prime Functions via manifested behaviors. You'll then be able to discern if those behavioral expressions are optimizing or detracting from your ability for wise living and overall wellbeing. If each or any of your brains are operating in suboptimal states, you'll know what needs to be facilitated within yourself so each brain can fulfill its Prime Function at the highest level.

In this exercise you will explore your strengths, patterns, habits and skill-gap opportunities in the core competencies of each of your brains. This will provide fruitful areas for you to work with your *m*BIT Coach to enhance your skills and bring more flexibility, freedom and choice to your world.

Core Competencies - Strengths

Heart Brain - Core Competencies

Predominantly Parasympathetic	<<	Balanced/Coherent	>>	Predominantly Sympathetic
Emotional Numbness	<<	**Peace/Forgiveness**	>>	Anger
Despair	<<	**Hope**	>>	Desperation
Sadness/Sorrow	<<	**Joy**	>>	Delirious/ Manic/Hysterical
Blind Trust	<<	**Trust**	>>	Distrust
Loneliness	<<	**Connection**	>>	Guarded
Emotionally Unaffected	<<	**Appreciation/ Gratitude**	>>	Obligation
Uncaring /Apathy	<<	**Compassion**	>>	Vengefulness
Emotionally Disengaged	<<	**Equanimity/ Emotional Security**	>>	Jealousy/Envy/ Emotional Insecurity
Indifference	<<	**Love**	>>	Hate
Self-focused	<<	**Generosity**	>>	Greed/Avarice
Emotional Blindness	<<	**Emotional Truth & Wisdom**	>>	Fickle/Lying Heart Emotional Deceit
Aimlessness	<<	**Passion (Dreams/Aspirations/ Values/Purpose)**	>>	Obsession

Gut Brain - Core Competencies

Predominantly Parasympathetic	<<	Balanced/Coherent	>>	Predominantly Sympathetic
Lust	<<	Hunger/Satiety	>>	Disgust
Sedation/ Hibernation	<<	Action/Gut Motivation/Drive	>>	Impulsiveness
Habit/Habituation	<<	Will-Power	>>	Compulsion/Urges
Fear-Freeze/Withdrawal	<<	Courage	>>	Fear-Fight/Flight
Lethargy/Depression	<<	Relaxed/Calm	>>	Anxiety
Self Preservation	<<	Wellbeing	>>	Self Damage
"Dumb shit"	<<	Gut Intuition	>>	Gut Turmoil

Head Brain - Core Competencies

Left hemisphere (Parasympathetic)	<<	Balanced/Coherent	>>	Right hemisphere (Sympathetic)
Orienting Through Time	<<	Being Present	>>	Atemporal
Dissociation	<<	Meta Consciousness/ Meta Cognition	>>	Subjective Reality
Singular Reality	<<	Balanced Perspective/ Integrated View	>>	Simultaneous Multiple Realities
Mental-Efforting and Struggle	<<	Flow States	>>	Mental/Subjective Drifting
Convergent Thinking	<<	Creativity	>>	Divergent Thinking
Fixation	<<	Curiosity	>>	Mentally Scattered
Logical-Structured Learning	<<	Transformational/ Generative Learning	>>	Survival/ Streetwise Learning

On the frameworks listed on the previous pages, for each of the brains:

 Mark or tick any and all of the competencies you believe or feel you are strongest in, are '*good*' at, skilled in, or get the most benefit from in your life. Which of these competencies that you've ticked are your three top strengths overall? For each brain, which competency is your strongest? Which autonomic mode do your competencies sit in? Are there any discernable patterns here?

[Note that something you are skilled or '*unconsciously competent*' in may not necessarily produce positive results. This exercise is about exploring and determining the core competencies you are very skilled in, both those that you feel are positive and those that aren't so positive for your life.]

Core Competencies - Skill-gaps and Opportunities

Heart Brain - Core Competencies

Predominantly Parasympathetic	<<	Balanced/Coherent	>>	Predominantly Sympathetic
Emotional Numbness	<<	**Peace/Forgiveness**	>>	Anger
Despair	<<	**Hope**	>>	Desperation
Sadness/Sorrow	<<	**Joy**	>>	Delirious/ Manic/Hysterical
Blind Trust	<<	**Trust**	>>	Distrust
Loneliness	<<	**Connection**	>>	Guarded
Emotionally Unaffected	<<	**Appreciation/ Gratitude**	>>	Obligation
Uncaring /Apathy	<<	**Compassion**	>>	Vengefulness
Emotionally Disengaged	<<	**Equanimity/ Emotional Security**	>>	Jealousy/Envy/ Emotional Insecurity
Indifference	<<	**Love**	>>	Hate
Self-focused	<<	**Generosity**	>>	Greed/Avarice
Emotional Blindness	<<	**Emotional Truth & Wisdom**	>>	Fickle/Lying Heart Emotional Deceit
Aimlessness	<<	**Passion (Dreams/Aspirations/ Values/Purpose)**	>>	Obsession

Gut Brain - Core Competencies

Predominantly Parasympathetic	<<	Balanced/Coherent	>>	Predominantly Sympathetic
Lust	<<	Hunger/Satiety	>>	Disgust
Sedation/ Hibernation	<<	Action/Gut Motivation/Drive	>>	Impulsiveness
Habit/Habituation	<<	Will-Power	>>	Compulsion/Urges
Fear-Freeze/Withdrawal	<<	Courage	>>	Fear-Fight/Flight
Lethargy/Depression	<<	Relaxed/Calm	>>	Anxiety
Self Preservation	<<	Wellbeing	>>	Self Damage
"Dumb shit"	<<	Gut Intuition	>>	Gut Turmoil

Head Brain - Core Competencies

Left hemisphere (Parasympathetic)	<<	Balanced/Coherent	>>	Right hemisphere (Sympathetic)
Orienting Through Time	<<	Being Present	>>	Atemporal
Dissociation	<<	Meta Consciousness/ Meta Cognition	>>	Subjective Reality
Singular Reality	<<	Balanced Perspective/ Integrated View	>>	Simultaneous Multiple Realities
Mental-Efforting and Struggle	<<	Flow States	>>	Mental/Subjective Drifting
Convergent Thinking	<<	Creativity	>>	Divergent Thinking
Fixation	<<	Curiosity	>>	Mentally Scattered
Logical-Structured Learning	<<	Transformational/ Generative Learning	>>	Survival/ Streetwise Learning

On the frameworks listed on the previous pages, for each of the brains:

 Mark or circle any and all of the competencies you believe or feel you are weakest in, have the most challenges with, or get the most problems or issues with in your life. Which of these competencies that you have circled are your three biggest challenges overall? For each brain, which competency is your most problematic? Which Autonomic mode are these competencies in? Are there any discernable patterns here?

Core Competencies – Habitual Preferences

Heart Brain - Core Competencies

Predominantly Parasympathetic	<<	Balanced/Coherent	>>	Predominantly Sympathetic
Emotional Numbness	<<	Peace/Forgiveness	>>	Anger
Despair	<<	Hope	>>	Desperation
Sadness/Sorrow	<<	Joy	>>	Delirious/ Manic/Hysterical
Blind Trust	<<	Trust	>>	Distrust
Loneliness	<<	Connection	>>	Guarded
Emotionally Unaffected	<<	Appreciation/ Gratitude	>>	Obligation
Uncaring /Apathy	<<	Compassion	>>	Vengefulness
Emotionally Disengaged	<<	Equanimity/ Emotional Security	>>	Jealousy/Envy/ Emotional Insecurity
Indifference	<<	Love	>>	Hate
Self-focused	<<	Generosity	>>	Greed/Avarice
Emotional Blindness	<<	Emotional Truth & Wisdom	>>	Fickle/Lying Heart Emotional Deceit
Aimlessness	<<	Passion (Dreams/Aspirations/ Values/Purpose)	>>	Obsession

Gut Brain - Core Competencies

Predominantly Parasympathetic	<<	Balanced/Coherent	>>	Predominantly Sympathetic
Lust	<<	Hunger/Satiety	>>	Disgust
Sedation/ Hibernation	<<	Action/Gut Motivation/Drive	>>	Impulsiveness
Habit/Habituation	<<	Will-Power	>>	Compulsion/Urges
Fear-Freeze/Withdrawal	<<	Courage	>>	Fear-Fight/Flight
Lethargy/Depression	<<	Relaxed/Calm	>>	Anxiety
Self Preservation	<<	Wellbeing	>>	Self Damage
"Dumb shit"	<<	Gut Intuition	>>	Gut Turmoil

Head Brain - Core Competencies

Left hemisphere (Parasympathetic)	<<	Balanced/Coherent	>>	Right hemisphere (Sympathetic)
Orienting Through Time	<<	Being Present	>>	Atemporal
Dissociation	<<	Meta Consciousness/ Meta Cognition	>>	Subjective Reality
Singular Reality	<<	Balanced Perspective/ Integrated View	>>	Simultaneous Multiple Realities
Mental-Efforting and Struggle	<<	Flow States	>>	Mental/Subjective Drifting
Convergent Thinking	<<	Creativity	>>	Divergent Thinking
Fixation	<<	Curiosity	>>	Mentally Scattered
Logical-Structured Learning	<<	Transformational/ Generative Learning	>>	Survival/ Streetwise Learning

On the frameworks listed on the previous pages, for each of the brains:

 Mark or circle any and all of the competencies you do the most, the ones that are habitual and/or typical preferences. Which autonomic mode are these competencies in? Is there any discernable pattern here? How do these patterns serve you or create issues for you? How do these patterns compare to those you marked in the earlier Strengths and Skill-gaps sections of this exercise? What insights come to mind from this?

What competencies are missing from the Balanced mode (center) column of your list? What competencies would you like to do more of? What would make a positive wiser difference to your life?

Generative Learning: Future Pacing the next *m*BIT Coaching Session

Reflections and Learnings

Points to discuss at the next session

Coaching outcomes I'd like to pursue/explore

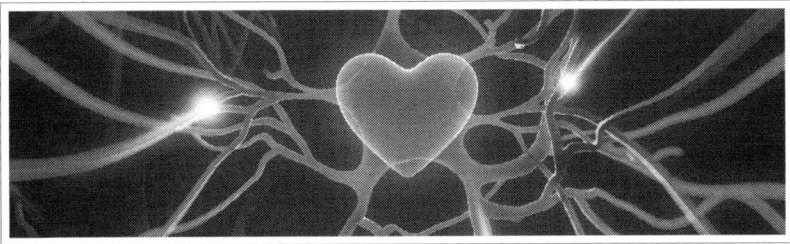

8.

Congruence and Alignment

Congruence is '*the quality or state of agreeing, matching and harmony*,' it's when all parts of you line up and are in agreement. In large measure, this is about alignment between your multiple brains. What happens when your heart passionately tells you one thing, but your gut violently disagrees? Or when your head is at odds with the messages from either your heart or gut? Have you ever found yourself fighting amongst these parts of your mind? If you have, you aren't alone. Our behavioral modeling research suggests this is an all too common experience.

The flip side of this is to eliminate any conflict between the brains, and ensure they are in agreement and supporting each other in their functions toward a common outcome. Incongruence or mismatch between the multiple brains undermines resolve, causes confusion and ultimately leads to incongruent behaviors and outcomes. You literally sabotage your own success. We've all had experiences of this, either in our own lives, or in the people around us. Think of times when you've felt torn on a decision, where one part of you has agreed but another part has not. How did that work out? Probably not as well as it could…

So for success in life you need all parts of your self, all of your brains, congruently aligned and supporting your success.

The world reflects your processes back to you

You know, it's not just about what's happening in your own multiple brains either. Incongruence within and between your brains is usually embodied and expressed (typically outside of conscious awareness) in your physical stance, your micro-muscle movements, your facial expressions and your non-verbal communication. So any incongruence you're feeling is non-verbally expressed to other people's unconscious minds and undermines your chances of success with them. This is how self-fulfilling prophecies work within human relationships. We literally express and communicate all the messages from our multiple brains, and get responses from others that recapitulate our expectations.

As an example, if someone is sending out mixed messages, you'll feel it in your gut or heart as an instinct not to trust the person. This in turn influences your own decisions and behaviors and you'll end up reflecting back that lack of trust. This can amplify in a loop of mutual distrust and cause problems in how you work or relate together.

So congruence is vital for both working with your self and with others. Success and ultimately wisdom in all your outcomes and behaviors requires alignment and congruence at every level.

Incongruence Signals

If the three brains are not in alignment or congruent with one another over an issue, any incongruence will show up as observable behavioral indicators, signs and signals. Since the brains, mind and body are connected in a Cybernetic Loop of body-mind control, what affects one, affects them all and this leads to observable signals. With sufficient sensory acuity you can see and detect these signals.

Some of the classic incongruence signals include:

- Facial expressions of distaste or grimacing
- Asymmetrical expressions or gestures
- Hunching over or closing up
- Pupil constriction and narrowing of the eyes

- Turning or leaning away
- Gut and heart reactions or feelings
- Shaking of the head as if saying '*no*'
- Holding the breath, or short shallow breaths
- Quavering or hesitant voice tonalities
- Language indicators such as metaphors or expressions indicating non-alignment

Pay attention to these signals in your life and your behavior. If you see any sign of them make sure you discuss and explore them with your *m*BIT Coach and together you can work out what's going on, gain learnings from them and get coached in integrating and aligning all parts of yourself to support your ongoing success.

Congruence Exploration

 In what contexts or areas of your life do you believe you may lack congruence and alignment? Are there specific situations or people with whom you are out of harmony with or not fully aligned within your head, heart and gut about? In what contexts or situations do you do any of the following incongruence behaviors? What are the impacts of this in your life?

- Facial expressions of distaste or grimacing

- Asymmetrical expressions or gestures

- Hunching over or closing up

- Pupil constriction and narrowing of the eyes

- Turning or leaning away

- Gut and heart reactions or feelings

- Head-based confusion or conflicting thoughts

- Shaking of the head as if saying '*no*'

- Holding the breath, or short shallow breaths

- Quavering or hesitant voice tonalities

- Language indicators such as metaphors or expressions indicating non-alignment

- Saying one thing, but doing another

- Not following through on promises and commitments

What could you do to bring more congruence and alignment to your thoughts, feelings, actions, behaviors, decisions and ways of being etc.? How can you become more aware of your incongruence signals and triggers? How can you support yourself to be even more wisely congruent and aligned, and to bring more Compassion, Creativity and Courage to being at one with yourself?

What would a more congruent and aligned you be like? What would this feel like? What will you do differently? What specific actions will a more congruent you take in life, and how will this make a difference for you and others?

Generative Learning: Future Pacing the next *m*BIT Coaching Session

Reflections and Learnings

Points to discuss at the next session

Coaching outcomes I'd like to pursue/explore

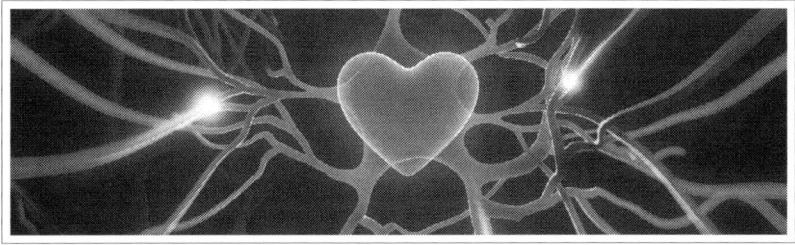

9.

Highest Expressions

Highest Expressions are the most adaptive and generative virtues or competencies of each of your brains. The highest expression of the heart brain is Compassion, for the gut brain it is Courage and for the head it's Creativity.

In this section of the Workbook you will explore each of these Highest Expressions, looking for patterns and behaviors that limit you or hold you back in truly living and embodying these competencies. Each of us has differing strengths and patterns or preferences in how we use our brains. By understanding more about your own behavioral patterns and tendencies, you can work with your *m*BIT Coach to strengthen the areas in which you have weaknesses, blind-spots or dysfunctional patterns. And most importantly, focus on improving those areas that may be holding you back from truly becoming all that you can be and do in your life, from becoming the Highest Expression of you!

Highest Expression Strengths

On a scale of 0 to 5, where 0 is no skill whatsoever and 5 represents the most skill you can imagine, rate yourself in how well you are able to do each of the Highest Expressions.

Compassion (place a circle or X below to rate your level of skill and competence)

(No Skill) **0** - - - - - **1** - - - - - **2** - - - - - **3** - - - - - **4** - - - - - **5** (Magnificent Skill)

Creativity (place a circle or X below to rate your level of skill and competence)

(No Skill) **0** - - - - - **1** - - - - - **2** - - - - - **3** - - - - - **4** - - - - - **5** (Magnificent Skill)

Courage (place a circle or X below to rate your level of skill and competence)

(No Skill) **0** - - - - - **1** - - - - - **2** - - - - - **3** - - - - - **4** - - - - - **5** (Magnificent Skill)

Note which of the Highest Expressions you are strongest in and weakest in?

Now in the following sections, explore questions about each of the Highest Expressions in detail.

Compassion Exploration

What are the components and skills of compassion? Do a mindmap of these.

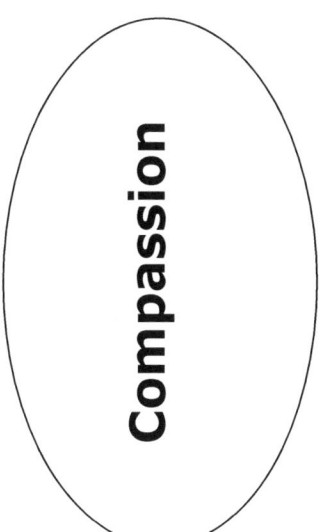

Compassion Exploration

 In what contexts or areas of your life do you believe you may lack compassion for others? Are there specific situations or people? What are the impacts of this in your life? In what contexts or areas of your life do you easily do great compassion? What is the difference?

In what contexts or areas of your life do you believe you may lack compassion for yourself? Are there specific situations that trigger this? What are the impacts of this in your life? In what contexts or areas of your life do you easily do great compassion for your self? What is the difference?

In what situations do you feel or experience compassion but not take action? What could you do to change that?

Are there any examples, people or contexts with which you act compassionately but it ends up being *'dumb compassion'* i.e. it causes more issues and problems than you thought or felt it would?

What could you do to bring wiser compassion to your actions, decisions and ways of being etc.? How can you bring more caring, kindness, consideration, empathy and aligned compassion to your life?

What would a more compassionate you be like? What would this feel like? What will you do differently? What specific actions will a more compassionate you take in life, and how will this have made a difference for you and others?

Generative Learning: Future Pacing the next *m*BIT Coaching Session

Reflections and Learnings

Points to discuss at the next session

Coaching outcomes I'd like to pursue/explore

Creativity Exploration

What are the components and skills of creativity? Do a mindmap of these.

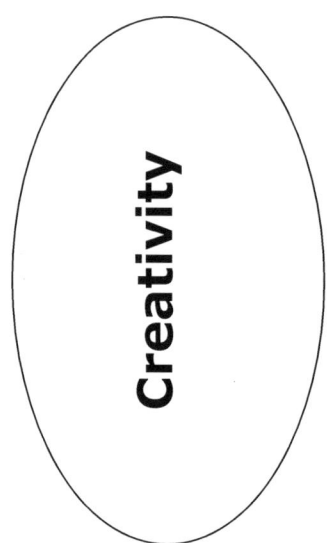

Creativity Exploration

 In what contexts or areas of your life do you believe you may lack positive creativity? Are there specific situations, contexts or issues in which you need to be or can become more creative in your internal and external responses? Are there contexts or situations in which you are creative but it is *'negative'* creativity and you'd like to turn this around to create more positive and generative results? In what contexts or areas of your life are you magnificently creative? What is the difference?

What could you do to bring more positive and wiser creativity to your thoughts, decisions, actions, and ways of being etc.? How can you bring more novelty, possibility and integrated creativity to your life?

In what situations do you feel or experience positive creativity but not actually take action to tangibly manifest your creative thoughts into the world? What could you do to change that?

What would a more creative you be like? What would this feel like? What will you do differently? What specific actions will a more creative you take in life, and what will then open up and have become possible for you and your life?

Generative Learning: Future Pacing the next *m*BIT Coaching Session

Reflections and Learnings

Points to discuss at the next session

Coaching outcomes I'd like to pursue/explore

Courage Exploration

What are the components and skills of courage? Do a mindmap of these.

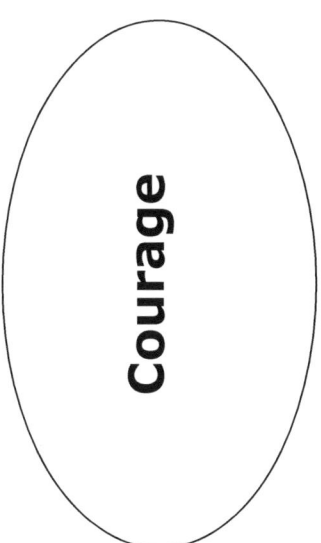

Courage Exploration

 In what contexts or areas of your life do you believe you may lack courage? Are there specific situations or particular people you need to be more courageous with and for? How does this impact your life? In what contexts or areas of your life do you do incredible courage? What is the difference?

In what situations do you feel or experience fear but not take gutsy action? What prevents you from taking courageous action despite the fear sensations? How does this impact your life and your sense of who you are? In what situations or contexts do you push through fear and take gutsy action? What is the difference?

What could you do to bring wiser courage to your actions, decisions and ways of being etc.? What are the ways you have motivated yourself in the past to do courage and overcome fear (e.g. anger), but that you could now do in a wiser more generative way? How can you bring more gutsy motivated and wise courage to your life?

What would a more courageous you be like? What would this feel like? What will you do differently? What specific actions would a more courageous you take in life, and how will your life have become different?

Generative Learning: Future Pacing the next *m*BIT Coaching Session

Reflections and Learnings

Points to discuss at the next session

Coaching outcomes I'd like to pursue/explore

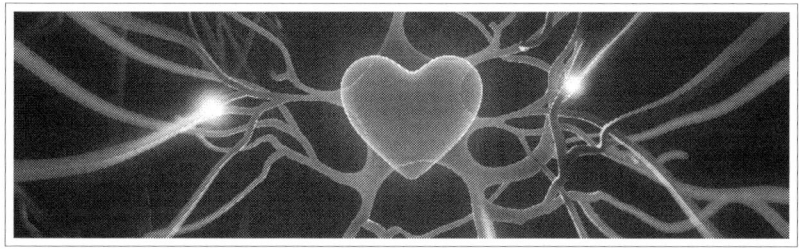

10.

Highest Expression Integration

Integrating across Prime Functions

The Highest Expressions of Compassion, Creativity and Courage are integrative, each requires the others in order to do its wisest expression. They are also integrative across the Prime Functions. For example, at the heart level, you can do joy as a competency, but you could do a form of joy that is all about your own values and emotions and doesn't take into account relational affect – a joy that is selfishly motivated and doesn't give a care for the feelings of others. So joy as a heart competency doesn't have to be integrated across all the Prime Functions of the heart brain. However, compassion as a Highest Expression is integrated across all Prime Functions. You cannot do a selfish version of wise compassion. Compassion values others, has positive feelings towards others and deeply connects you with others. In other words, compassion utilizes all of the Prime Functions of the heart in wise ways.

For true Highest Expression integration, you need all of the Highest Expressions integrated and wisely utilizing all of the Prime Functions across all of the brains. So in the case of compassion, you'd need to ensure that compassion also involves compassionate cognitive perceptions, thoughts and meaning (head brain) and compassionate motility/action, self-preservation and core identity (gut brain).

In this exercise, you'll explore how your ways of doing and living the Highest Expressions integrate across all of your brains and all of their Prime Functions. This is quite a complex exercise and may get a little confusing, so you may want to do an initial exploration of it with your *m*BIT Coach to get you started. However, the more deeply you can explore your patterns across Highest Expression integration, the more powerfully you can begin to live in a way that is adaptive, generative and integrative.

Prime Function Integration Exploration

Head: Creativity	Heart: Compassion	Gut: Courage
• Cognitive Perception	• Emoting	• Mobilization / Action
• Thinking	• Relational Affect / Connecting with Others	• Self-Preservation
• Making Meaning	• Values	• Core Identity

Looking at the chart above of the brains, their Highest Expressions and the Prime Functions of each, map or note any areas in which you feel you are not fully integrating across or between your brains and Prime Functions.

For example, you may feel you are creative in your thinking and the other head based functions, but you are not creative in how you relate and connect with others, or how you take action and mobilize in your day to day life. Or you may feel that you are very compassionate in how you deal with other people, but not in how you deal with yourself at a gut based core identity level or how you look after yourself (self-preservation).

Draw some lines around or between areas of potential weakness, points of interest or concern that you'd like to discuss with your *m*BIT Coach, and number them. Then write some notes below that link to the numbered items, with your thoughts, feelings and ideas.

Thoughts/Feelings/Notes/Points for Discussion:

Generative Learning: Future Pacing the next *m*BIT Coaching Session

Reflections and Learnings

Points to discuss at the next session

Coaching outcomes I'd like to pursue/explore

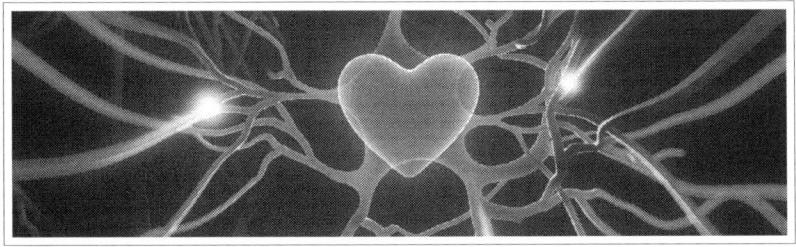

11.

Trust Patterns

"Without trust there is nothing."

If there is no trust between each of your brains then you can forget true alignment and integration. If your head doesn't trust your heart, or your heart doesn't trust your gut, the lack of trust will undermine congruence and cause blocking of messages and integration between the brains. It's really no different from how you treat someone in your own life that you distrust completely. You'll ignore or discredit the things they tell you, thinking that it's just more lies.

There is a structure to the process of trust, and in order to build trust between the brains, you need to understand that structure and find the points of failure in the process and remedy them. As you rebuild trust, only then can you fully coach the three brains into congruence, agreement and alignment.

Trust between your brains involves four key components:

- Communication
- Caring
- Consistency
- Competency

In the following exercises you will explore the patterns of trust in both your life and between your multiple brains. By becoming aware of and understanding your patterns and blocks to trusting, you can start to build more generative and wiser ways of trusting in your relationships, both within yourself and with others. This is an exceptionally fruitful area for working with your *m*BIT Coach.

Exploring Trust Patterns

 In what contexts or areas of your life do you experience trouble with trusting, in which you may lack trust for others, or suffer due to a lack of trust (or perhaps even over-trust)? Are there specific situations or people you have trust issues with? What are the impacts of this in your life?

In what contexts or areas of your life do you experience trouble with trusting yourself? Are there any ways in which you lack trust for yourself, or suffer due to a lack of trust in yourself (or perhaps even over-trust)? Are there specific situations you have trust issues with? What are the impacts of this in your life?

Do you completely trust your head? Do you fully trust your heart? Do you deeply trust your gut? If not, in what contexts or situations do you not trust one or all of your brains? What impact does this have on your life?

 In your relationship with your self, between your three brains or even between yourself and others, what issues do you have with:

Communication?

Caring?

Consistency?

Competency?

Generative Learning: Future Pacing the next *m*BIT Coaching Session

Reflections and Learnings

Points to discuss at the next session

Coaching outcomes I'd like to pursue/explore

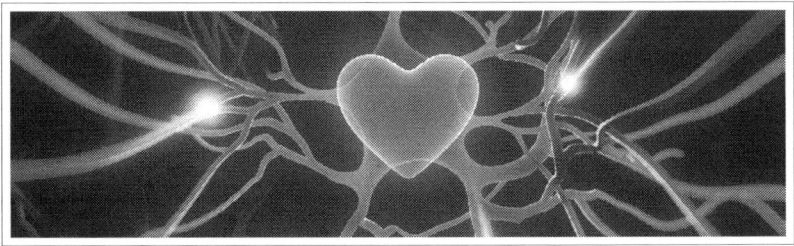

12.

Neural Integration Blocks (NIB's) Patterns

There are times while aligning your head, heart and gut brain, that one or more of your neural networks will block the process of integration. They just won't respond or allow the integration message through. We call these blocks Neural Integration Blocks (NIB's) and in our behavioral modeling work we've found a number of ways that NIB's occur. In this section, you'll explore patterns and processes of blocking that may or may not occur in your life. Note that not everyone experiences NIB's, so you may not find answers to the following exercises, however, it can be very powerful and useful to uncover those that exist, and provide fruitful areas for you to work with your *m*BIT Coach.

To give you something to work with, the following lists summarize how the brains can do blocking. For further info or details about this please refer to *mBraining* Chapter 6 or speak to your *m*BIT Coach to go through this with you.

How the heart can do NIB'ing

The heart brain can block integration through typical emotional and physical responses of:

1. Lethargy or apathy

2. Heart palpitations

3. Heart *'freak out'*

4. Emotional shut down, emotional stonewalling

5. Anger

6. Emotional defensiveness and over-sensitivity

How the gut can do NIB'ing

The gut brain predominantly blocks through the use of:

1. Armoring

2. Nausea, throwing up, pushing back, etc.

3. Scatological marking

4. Distraction (churning, dizziness, spinning, etc.)

How the head can do NIB'ing

The head brain has a huge array of blocking strategies it can use. These include:

1. Blaming

2. Justifying and rationalizing

3. Denying

4. Confusion

5. Smoke screening

6. Overwhelm

7. Going blank

8. Bolstering

9. Identification

10. Arguing for limitations

11. Insistence on not knowing ("I don't know, I don't know!")

12. Meta-commenting (explain it away, or explaining yourself right back into your current situation)

13. Double-binds

14. Quitting

Exploring Your Neural Integration Block Patterns

 Do you have any situations or issues in which your head, heart and gut are typically not aligned or are refusing to connect or agree on? Are there any patterns of this that re-occur for you over time?

Are there any contexts, people or situations that cause you to disconnect, dissociate or withdraw from? How does this impact your life?

Are there any contexts, people or situations that are causing arguments, discomfort or disagreement between your head, heart and gut, or are having negative impacts, harmful results or unintended negative consequences and you are impacted by this at a head, heart or gut level?

Generative Learning: Future Pacing the next *m*BIT Coaching Session

Reflections and Learnings

Points to discuss at the next session

Coaching outcomes I'd like to pursue/explore

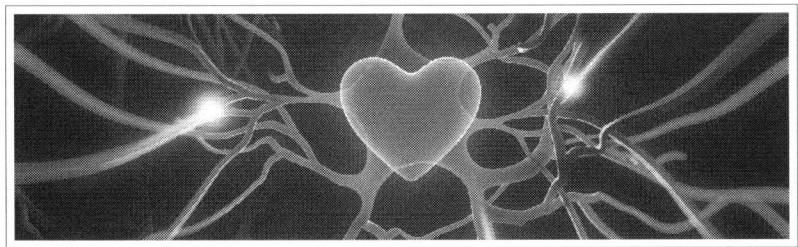

13.

Cognitive Dissonance Patterns

In 1956, Stanford University psychologist Leon Festinger heard about a group of doomsday cultists who were predicting the Earth would be destroyed by aliens at midnight on December 21st of that year. Festinger and his students decided to infiltrate the group and covertly study what happens to people when their strongly held beliefs are disproved. What he discovered lead to the powerful and informative theory of Cognitive Dissonance.

So what did happen, in the minutes and hours after midnight, when the prophesied destruction and the predicted appearance of alien spacecraft to save the faithful didn't occur? Initially there was shock and disbelief by the members of the group; many had left jobs, colleges and spouses to prepare to escape on the flying saucer supposed to rescue them. Within hours however, people began to deny they'd ever believed in the doomsday prophecy. They were saying things like "I didn't really believe it, I was just going along for the adventure." Or, "Because of our strong faith, the aliens chose to save the planet." Basically, they said and thought anything other than the truth which was that they'd been duped all along.

Based on this research and thousands of subsequent laboratory and real-world studies, Festinger posited his theory that the unconscious mind does not like '*dissonance*' and will do anything to remove it. Dissonance is the disagreeable visceral feeling we get when faced with mismatching cognitions or beliefs. Our mind likes harmony and congruence between our thoughts and beliefs and will utilize a number of unconscious strategies to remove cognitive dissonance. The tension of cognitive dissonance leads people to change either their beliefs and attitudes or their behavior.

The importance of this is that it leads people to denying reality and deleting or distorting their cognitions and perceptions. Cognitive dissonance can be incredibly damaging if it leads to denial of reality and bizarre distortions or behaviors. Of course, cognitive dissonance is like any tool or process; it can be used positively or negatively.

For example, you can use cognitive dissonance and your multiple brains' response to it to motivate and assist you in creating generative change in your life by positively aligning your thoughts, values and actions. However, when cognitive dissonance occurs outside your conscious awareness it can minimize the quality of how you experience your life and lead you into ignorance.

Cognitive Dissonance Strategies

So in summary, cognitive dissonance is an uncomfortable feeling caused by holding conflicting ideas simultaneously. It is usually felt in the gut or chest region, though it can be felt in the head as well. Typically, the tension of cognitive dissonance leads people to change either their beliefs and attitudes or their behavior through the unconscious strategies of:

1. **Avoidance** — people avoid information that is likely to lead to dissonance

2. **Distortion** — people delete and distort facts and beliefs to reduce dissonance

3. **Confirmation** — people are attracted to or perform selective bias on information that confirms or bolsters their cognitions

4. **Reassurance** — people look for reassurance from others that their cognitions and beliefs are correct and ok

5. **Re-valuation** — people change the importance of existing and new ideas, facts and cognitions to reduce dissonance

Understanding and tracking these processes is an important component of self-awareness. While cognitive dissonance often leads people into denying reality or deleting and distorting their cognitions and perceptions, it doesn't need to be that way. When you're aware that your brains don't like mismatching ideas, thoughts or beliefs, you can start to notice whenever dissonance occurs and accept it as a natural response. You can then treat it as a valid signal coming from your head, heart or gut brains alerting you about mismatch in your internal world.

The very act of valuing cognitive dissonance as an awareness tool is itself a cognition and via bolstering leads to your unconscious mind not having to automatically delete or distort the mismatching cognitions. This process allows you to gain choice and control over how you are creating your cognitive world — the world of your beliefs, values, ideas and identity. In this way you can use cognitive dissonance as a tool for positively aligning your thoughts, values and behavior.

Cognitive dissonance also relates to decision-making. Research has shown that the more effort and time invested in a decision or the forming of a belief, the larger the potential dissonance created if mismatching evidence is discovered. The more important the outcome you are working with, the more likely your unconscious mind is to perform the above dissonance removal strategies. For example, if you purchase a low cost item, you're unlikely to experience buyer's remorse. However, for an expensive item you spent a lot of time evaluating, you're more likely to experience buyer's remorse and therefore more likely to go seeking confirmation and reassurance after the purchase. Awareness of these natural and inbuilt processes puts you at choice and allows you to wisely decide how you respond to life.

Exploring Your Cognitive Dissonance Patterns

 Think of a time when you experienced cognitive dissonance, when you were presented with facts that didn't fit your current beliefs and it created dissonance within you. What were the behavioral sensations and feelings? Thinking across a few situations of dissonance, where do you typically experience cognitive dissonance signals in your body? What are your indicators? How could you use this knowledge of your cognitive dissonance indicators to gain more choice in how you respond to dissonance?

? In what contexts, situations or with what people do you do the following patterns of cognitive dissonance removal? Are any of these strategies more prevalent for you? How does this impact your life?

Avoidance

Distortion

Confirmation

Reassurance

Re-valuation

What would be more useful and wiser ways to handle and overcome cognitive dissonance? What will a wiser you do in dissonant situations?

Generative Learning: Future Pacing the next *m*BIT Coaching Session

Reflections and Learnings

Points to discuss at the next session

Coaching outcomes I'd like to pursue/explore

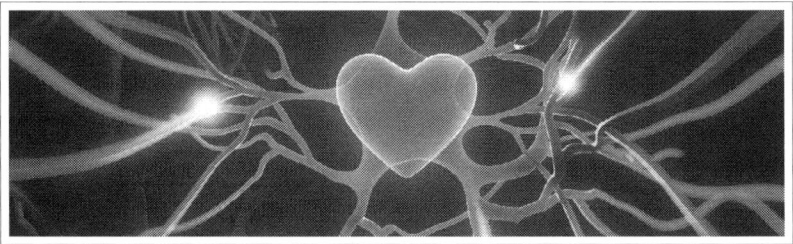

14.

*m*BIT Toolkit Category Patterns

While there are certainly many significant skill domains important for life success, from an *m*BIT perspective there are six vital areas of application most people experience some issues with at various times in their lives. Learning and applying *m*BIT processes to these domains can make a fundamental difference to the quality of your life and the results you're achieving. The *m*BIT Toolkit domains that are useful to explore are:

1. Self-awareness & Evolving your intuition

2. State management & Self-control

3. Courage, Motivation & Action-taking

4. Decision-making & Problem-solving

5. Habit control & Overcoming compulsions

6. Health & Wellbeing

Each of the domains builds on and utilizes the ones before it. Your ability for example to do courage and motivation requires skills and expertise in state management and self-control. These in turn depend upon self-awareness and deep intuition so you can tap deeply into your unconscious signals and processes that are used in state management.

So in the following exercises you'll explore your levels of perceived skills in these domains and determine your strengths, weaknesses and patterns in each of the domains. You can then work with your *m*BIT Coach to refine your skills, to align and bring greater wisdom to each of the domains and to add greater value to your life through re-patterning where appropriate.

Toolkit Category Strengths

On a scale of 0 to 5, where 0 is no skill whatsoever and 5 represents the most skill you can imagine, rate yourself in how well you are able to do each of the Toolkit domains.

Self-awareness & Intuition (place a circle or X below to rate your level of skill and competence)

(No Skill) **0** - - - - - **1** - - - - - **2** - - - - - **3** - - - - - **4** - - - - - **5** (Magnificent Skill)

State management & Self-control (place a circle or X below to rate your level of skill and competence)

(No Skill) **0** - - - - - **1** - - - - - **2** - - - - - **3** - - - - - **4** - - - - - **5** (Magnificent Skill)

Courage, Motivation & Action-taking (place a circle or X below to rate your level of skill and competence)

(No Skill) **0** - - - - - **1** - - - - - **2** - - - - - **3** - - - - - **4** - - - - - **5** (Magnificent Skill)

Decision-making & Problem-solving (place a circle or X below to rate your level of skill and competence)

(No Skill) **0** - - - - - **1** - - - - - **2** - - - - - **3** - - - - - **4** - - - - - **5** (Magnificent Skill)

Habit control & Overcoming compulsions (place a circle or X below to rate your level of skill and competence)

(No Skill) **0** - - - - - **1** - - - - - **2** - - - - - **3** - - - - - **4** - - - - - **5** (Magnificent Skill)

Health & Well-being (place a circle or X below to rate your level of skill and competence)

(No Skill) **0** - - - - - **1** - - - - - **2** - - - - - **3** - - - - - **4** - - - - - **5** (Magnificent Skill)

Self-awareness & Intuition

 In what contexts or areas of your life do you believe you may lack self-awareness or intuition? Are there specific situations or particular people you need to be more intuitive with and for? What might you become more self-aware of? Do you trust your intuition? How does this impact your life?

In what situations do you experience intuitive messages or signals from your mind and body, your head, heart or gut, but ignore them or downplay them? What prevents you from taking your intuitions seriously and acting upon them? How does this impact your life and your sense of who you are?

What could you do to bring more wisdom to your self-awareness and your attending to and trusting your intuitions? What difference would this make to your life?

What would a more self-aware and intuitive you be like? What would this feel like? What will you do differently? What specific actions will a more aware and intuitive you take in life, and how will your life have become different from this?

Generative Learning: Future Pacing the next *m*BIT Coaching Session

Reflections and Learnings

Points to discuss at the next session

Coaching outcomes I'd like to pursue/explore

State management & Self-control

 In what contexts or areas of your life do you believe you may lack state management and self-control? Are there specific situations or particular people you need to exert more self-control with? How does this impact your life?

Are there specific situations or particular people that you have forgiveness issues with? Are there specific situations or particular people that you have challenges with staying calm around? How skillful are you at letting go of things and calm-abiding the challenges that life throws at you? How does this impact your life and your sense of who you are?

How mindful are you of what is happening across and within your multiple brains (head, heart, gut)? Are there specific situations or particular people that impact on your ability to remain mindful? What could you do to bring more mindfulness to your thoughts, feelings, patterns and habits?

What would a more self-controlled and aligned you be like? What would it feel like to have more state management skills? What will you do differently? What specific actions will a more controlled and aligned you take in life, and how will your life have become different?

Generative Learning: Future Pacing the next *m*BIT Coaching Session

Reflections and Learnings

Points to discuss at the next session

Coaching outcomes I'd like to pursue/explore

Courage, Motivation & Action-taking

 In what contexts or areas of your life do you believe you may lack courage, motivation or the ability to take action? How does this impact your life?

Are there specific situations or particular people that trigger you to not push forward into your courage, to lose motivation or to stop taking action and getting moving? What prevents you from taking control in these situations? How does this impact your life and your sense of who you are?

What could you do to bring more wisdom to how you embody courage, motivate and encourage yourself, and congruently take action to achieve your goals, dreams and (wise) desires? Are there specific behaviors, thoughts, feelings and ways of being that help you to step into your courage, that help motivate you fully and compel you to take action?

What would a more courageous, motivated and action-oriented you be like? What would this feel like? What will you do differently? What specific actions will a more courageous, motivated and action-oriented you take in life, and how will your life have become different from this?

Generative Learning: Future Pacing the next *m*BIT Coaching Session

Reflections and Learnings

Points to discuss at the next session

Coaching outcomes I'd like to pursue/explore

Decision-making & Problem-solving

 Do you have any challenges with making decisions or solving problems in your life? Any behaviors around decision-making and problem-solving that don't serve you? In what contexts or areas of your life do you believe you may lack skills or abilities in decision-making and problem-solving? How does this impact your life?

Are there specific situations or particular people that trigger you to not be effective in making decisions or solving problems? What prevents you from doing more effective decision-making and problem-solving in these contexts? How does this impact your life and your sense of who you are?

What can you do to bring more wisdom to how you make decisions and solve problems?

What would a more effective decision-making and problem-solving you be like? What would this feel like? What will you do differently? What specific actions will you take in life, and how will your life have become different from this?

Generative Learning: Future Pacing the next *m*BIT Coaching Session

Reflections and Learnings

Points to discuss at the next session

Coaching outcomes I'd like to pursue/explore

Habit control & Overcoming compulsions

 Do you have any unwanted habits or compulsions you'd like to change? Any compulsive behaviors that no longer serve you? In what contexts or areas of your life do you believe you may lack sufficient habit control or choice? How does this impact your life?

In what situations do you experience compulsions? Are there specific situations or particular people that trigger compulsive or negative habits or behaviors? What are the hidden-benefits or underlying needs that the compulsive habits and behaviors are trying to fulfill? What prevents you from controlling these unwanted reactions or behaviors? How does this impact your life and your sense of who you are?

What can you do to bring more wisdom to how you notice and respond to compulsive desires or negative and un-useful patterns and habits?

What would a more controlled and aligned you be like? What would this feel like? What will you do differently? What specific actions will a more controlled and aligned you take in life, and how will your life have become different from this?

Generative Learning: Future Pacing the next *m*BIT Coaching Session

Reflections and Learnings

Points to discuss at the next session

Coaching outcomes I'd like to pursue/explore

Health & Well-being

 In what contexts or areas of your life do you lack, or not have optimum health and well-being? Do you have as much energy, wellness and resilience as you'd like? What thoughts, feelings or behaviors do you do that decease or impact your health and wellness? Are there specific situations, contexts or particular people that impact your health behaviors? What health and wellness patterns do you have in your life that don't serve you? How does this impact your life?

In what situations do you experience health and wellness signals from your mind and body but ignore them or downplay them? What prevents you from taking your health and wellness seriously and acting upon it? How does this impact your life and your sense of who you are?

What could you do to bring more wisdom to your health and wellness processes? What thoughts, feelings or behaviors do you do that increase or enhance your health and wellness, and bring you more vitality? How can you do more of these?

What would a more healthy, energetic and vibrant you be like? What would this feel like? What will you do differently? What specific actions will a more healthy and vital you take in life, and how will your life have become different from this?

Generative Learning: Future Pacing the next *m*BIT Coaching Session

Reflections and Learnings

Points to discuss at the next session

Coaching outcomes I'd like to pursue/explore

15.

mBraining Discovery Exercises

This section provides a copy of the Discovery Exercises found throughout the *mBraining* book. Your *m*BIT Coach may task you with completing some of these exercises so that you gain more personal experience in various aspects of the processes of *mBraining*.

Exploring the Prime Functions

In this exercise you explore and discover the prime functions of your three brains (head, hear and gut) and how they operate in your world.

1. As you read the following statements, work out where each of these is processed and experienced in your body, and which is the main operating intelligence/brain:

   - I really need to think this one through
   - I swallowed my fear and got moving
   - I understand what you're saying more clearly now
   - I really love that
   - It was a gutsy and courageous thing to do
   - What's the logic behind that?
   - I really appreciate what you did for me
   - I really want to forgive her
   - I'm fed up with it, enough is enough

   Did you notice that the different statements evoked different qualities of responses within you and that these responses originated in the regions corresponding with the appropriate brain?

2. Remember a time when you were:

   - Gutsy and courageous

   Take a moment and fully re-experience this. Now, remember a time when you were:

   - Filled with love and kindness

   Take another moment to fully re-experience this. And now, remember a time when you were:

   - Logical and clear headed

   Notice what's different in your subjective experience between the three scenarios. Notice the difference in '*what*' you are processing. Now notice what's different in '*how*' you are processing them. Finally, notice the location in your body of '*where*' you are processing them.

With even a moderate degree of self-awareness most people are able to sense the differences between these three experiences. If you are one of the small number of people who are not able to detect any difference then you will benefit greatly from the Awareness Exercises throughout the book.

3. Think of a decision you've made where there were several complex factors to consider but you made an effective decision anyway. Become aware of which of the intelligences you used to make the final decision. Was the ultimate decision based only on head logic? Did you go with your heart? Or was it your gut instinct that had the final call? And was there a consensus between all your brains?

    Now contrast that with a decision that didn't go well in the end. One where it seemed like a good idea at the time, but with the benefit of hindsight you now realize you made a poor decision. Which of your brains was involved in that and in what sequence? Which intelligence did you not listen to or attend to? Is there a difference in this situation compared to the successful decision?

Notes/Thoughts/Insights:

Core Competencies Self-awareness

In this discovery exercise you'll learn to use the core *mBrain* competencies framework as a tool for self-awareness around how your brains are functioning in a real life context.

Awareness

1. Identify a goal, decision or issue you are having a challenge with.

2. Become aware of your subjective experience and take an inventory of what is occurring for you in your head, heart and gut.

3. Put a word label on your main subjective experience (e.g. sad, confused, scared, etc.). You may have several words to describe your overall state as one, two or all three of your intelligences may be actively expressing themselves regarding your issue.

Discovery

4. Look through the core *mBrain* competencies listings (below) and find the competency(s) that match or come closest to matching your word label(s).

5. Note which intelligence(s)/brain(s) your issue resides in, and do a self-assessment on which prime function it is trying to fulfill. If your issue spans more than one brain, reflect on the nature of the conflict occurring between the two intelligences and the related prime functions. What insights can you glean here?

Diagnosis

6. Now examine which modes are more dominant for the competencies in play. Are you functioning more in the sympathetic or parasympathetic mode? Reflect on this. What are the implications for being too aroused/stressed or too inhibited/withdrawn? Is this a pattern for you in other areas of your life with similar issues?

7. Explore options for how you might be able to activate your arousal or relaxation responses accordingly to counter-balance the current behavioral expressions (competencies) in play.

Balance

8. Identify the coherent/balanced state that is in the middle of the set that your currently active competency belongs to.

9. Explore what this coherent-balance state would be like for you in experience. Use this as a benchmark for you to manage your sympathetic-parasympathetic systems.

Notes/Thoughts/Insights:

Heart Brain - Core Competencies

Predominantly Parasympathetic	<<	Balanced/Coherent	>>	Predominantly Sympathetic
Emotional Numbness	<<	**Peace/Forgiveness**	>>	Anger
Despair	<<	**Hope**	>>	Desperation
Sadness/Sorrow	<<	**Joy**	>>	Delirious/ Manic/Hysterical
Blind Trust	<<	**Trust**	>>	Distrust
Loneliness	<<	**Connection**	>>	Guarded
Emotionally Unaffected	<<	**Appreciation/ Gratitude**	>>	Obligation
Uncaring /Apathy	<<	**Compassion**	>>	Vengefulness
Emotionally Disengaged	<<	**Equanimity/ Emotional Security**	>>	Jealousy/Envy/ Emotional Insecurity
Indifference	<<	**Love**	>>	Hate
Self-focused	<<	**Generosity**	>>	Greed/Avarice
Emotional Blindness	<<	**Emotional Truth & Wisdom**	>>	Fickle/Lying Heart Emotional Deceit
Aimlessness	<<	**Passion (Dreams/Aspirations/ Values/Purpose)**	>>	Obsession

Gut Brain - Core Competencies

Predominantly Parasympathetic	<<	Balanced/Coherent	>>	Predominantly Sympathetic
Lust	<<	Hunger/Satiety	>>	Disgust
Sedation/ Hibernation	<<	Action/Gut Motivation/Drive	>>	Impulsiveness
Habit/Habituation	<<	Will-Power	>>	Compulsion/Urges
Fear-Freeze/Withdrawal	<<	Courage	>>	Fear-Fight/Flight
Lethargy/Depression	<<	Relaxed/Calm	>>	Anxiety
Self Preservation	<<	Wellbeing	>>	Self Damage
"Dumb shit"	<<	Gut Intuition	>>	Gut Turmoil

Head Brain - Core Competencies

Left hemisphere (Parasympathetic)	<<	Balanced/Coherent	>>	Right hemisphere (Sympathetic)
Orienting Through Time	<<	Being Present	>>	Atemporal
Dissociation	<<	Meta Consciousness/ Meta Cognition	>>	Subjective Reality
Singular Reality	<<	Balanced Perspective/ Integrated View	>>	Simultaneous Multiple Realities
Mental-Efforting and Struggle	<<	Flow States	>>	Mental/Subjective Drifting
Convergent Thinking	<<	Creativity	>>	Divergent Thinking
Fixation	<<	Curiosity	>>	Mentally Scattered
Logical-Structured Learning	<<	Transformational/ Generative Learning	>>	Survival/ Streetwise Learning

Heart Awareness

In this discovery exercise you will learn to become aware of and tune into the beat of your heart.

Awareness (Basic)

1. Sit comfortably in a quiet space, take a moment to settle and breathe gently and evenly. As you continue to settle and relax, allow any thoughts and internal dialogue to arise naturally and just observe them as they come and go. Be a detached observer of your own internal processes, just let them arise then let them go.

2. As you are sitting, breathing gently, and continuing to relax, allow yourself to become more aware of your chest area. Breathe into your chest area and become aware of the sensations you can feel with each breath. Now begin to listen for, feel and track your heart beat in your upper chest.

3. Once you can get a sense of your heart beat, begin also to notice any other sensations and feelings in your heart and chest region.

4. Practice this exercise as often as you can, whenever you have a spare moment, the better you are at tuning in to your heart beat, the better you'll be at receiving the messages and intuitions from your heart brain.

Awareness (Contrast)

5. Sit comfortably and once again breathe gently as you become aware of your heart beat. Notice its rate, rhythm, and strength/intensity.

6. As you maintain this awareness, begin to recall or imagine a stressful situation. Notice any changes to your heart beat (rate, rhythm, strength/intensity) and any other sensations in your body.

7. Now let go of those stressful thoughts, internal images, and internal sounds/dialogue. Allow them to just float away while you focus on breathing gently. Notice any changes to your heart beat as you re-settle and re-center yourself.

8. As you maintain your awareness of your heartbeat, now recall or imagine a pleasant, happy memory or situation. Notice any changes to your heart beat (rate, rhythm, strength/intensity) and any other sensations in your body.

9. Once again, allow those thoughts, internal images, and internal sounds/dialogue to naturally float away. Focus on your gentle breathing and notice any changes to your heart beat as you become present to the here and now.

10. Practice becoming more aware of your heartbeat throughout the day during times of stress, enjoyment, and relaxation. This will develop your heart-based intuition and overall self-awareness.

Notes/Thoughts/Insights:

Balanced Breathing

In this discovery exercise you will learn to do coherent '*balanced breathing*' to put your heart and autonomic nervous system into a balanced, coherent state.

Preparation

1. Sit in a comfortable and relaxed position. (Note: do this in a sitting position rather than lying down).

2. Make sure your spine is straight and your shoulders are relaxed. Avoid having your tailbone tucked under you and your shoulders hunched forward as it will restrict your ability to breathe into your chest area. Instead, sit upright (without tension or effort), lengthen your spine, allow your shoulder blades to gently flatten against your back, and keep your head positioned over your shoulders (not protruding in front of them) to make sure your neck stays loose and relaxed.

3. Your eyes may be open or closed. Begin to breathe in deeply yet gently through the nose, and breathe out through either the nose or mouth, whichever is most comfortable. Do not use effort or force. Do this easily, naturally and in a relaxed manner.

4. While maintaining your relaxed and upright posture, breathe into and from your diaphragm. Feel your diaphragm naturally lower on the inhalation and naturally rise on the exhalation. Allow your deep yet gentle breath to also naturally expand your chest and ribcage area.

5. Combine the physical sensations of exhalation with feelings of deep relaxation. Do not force the exhalation. Exhale deeply without creating any tension in the torso. Maintain a relaxed and upright posture.

Balancing Your Breath

6. Now imagine an image of a sine wave in your mind. Imagine the sine wave spans a 12 second cycle, with approximately 6 seconds for the ascending part of the wave and 6 seconds for the descending part of the wave.

7. Imagine a ball moving along the sine wave and begin to breathe in sync with it. As it moves up the wave, gently inhale from your diaphragm for 6 seconds. As the ball moves down the wave, gently exhale from your diaphragm for 6 seconds. Try to make smooth transitions between inhalations and exhalations (and vice versa) as the ball moves around the top and bottom of this imaginary sine wave.

8. Remember to keep breathing from your diaphragm into your chest area. Keep your posture and spine upright and your shoulders and neck relaxed.

9. Continue balanced breathing in a deep yet relaxed manner for several minutes. The longer you can stay in a coherent state, the better. However even a couple of minutes in a coherent state has significant benefits. The mental, emotional and health benefits generated from this practice have been scientifically validated to be pervasive and long lasting.

Learning

10. Upon completion of this exercise, take some time to be aware of the changes in your mental, emotional and physical states as well as your overall state of being. Notice what is different in how you are experiencing your world and your ability to respond differently to whatever is presenting itself in the now.

Note: to help you we have created some breathing-pacer audio mp3 files, freely available at our website (www.mbraining.com) for you to download and use to pace your in-breaths and out-breaths.

Notes/Thoughts/Insights:

Amplifying With Emotions

In this discovery exercise you will learn to amplify your balanced breathing by breathing and communicating positive core emotions into your heart and communicating those messages to your head and gut brains.

1. Sit comfortably and begin the Balanced Breathing exercise described previously.

2. Once you have balanced your breathing for a few minutes along the '*sine wave pattern*' (breathing in for 6 seconds and out for 6 seconds), begin to think of a memory or imagine a scenario that produces strong positive emotions and feelings within you. This could be memories from your childhood, family, great achievements and celebrations, doing something you love or are passionate about, etc. Or they could be imagined scenarios of achieving future goals and aspirations, creative visualizations, '*what if*' and '*as if*' imaginings, etc.

3. Option: you may wish to also identify a language label for the positive emotion(s) and feeling(s) you are experiencing (e.g. love, happiness, peace, joy, etc). Some people find it useful to have a word label to use for the next steps in this exercise.

4. As you fully experience the positive emotions and feelings associated with your memory/imagined scenario, breathe into your heart area and feel your positive emotion filling your chest and heart area with each breath. Feel any tensions and non-complementary emotions leaving your body with each exhalation.

5. Still maintaining your balanced breathing, imagine and feel your positive emotion expanding upwards to your head brain. You may find it easier to start sending the signals upward with an in-breath.

6. As you continue to breathe from your heart up into your head, notice how your thoughts and perceptions change when they are connected to your heart and its positive emotion.

7. While maintaining this connection between your head and heart, breathe back down into your heart area.

8. Now continue to breathe the positive emotion from your heart down into your gut area. Feel your lower abdomen naturally expand as you inhale (you'll find that it helps greatly to keep a straight spine and to allow your pelvis to also move gently and naturally). Imagine and feel your positive emotion filling your lower abdomen/gut area.

9. Become aware of the changes to your sense of '*self*', e.g. changes in body sensations the releasing of muscular tensions, increased feelings of self-confidence and safety/security, and an upgrading of how you can '*be*' in this present moment.

10. As you fully experience the changes in your gut intelligence, breathe those changes back up into your heart. Allow each balanced breath to send the signals upwards from your gut to your heart, and feel the connection between these two brains.

11. Now breathe once again mainly into your heart area. With each balanced breath, experience your positive emotion flowing through the connections between your heart, head and gut brains. Expand that flow throughout your entire body and notice the changes in your overall wellbeing with an enhanced/expanded sense of who you are in the world.

Notes/Thoughts/Insights:

Swallowing a Smile

In this discovery exercise you'll learn to use swallowing to send a powerful message from your head to your gut brain. This exercise is derived from the powerful and insightful work of Grand Master Mantak Chia. It's based on ancient Taoist teachings and works through co-innervation of the esophagus with the head, heart and enteric nervous systems. You can find more detailed information on this technique and many others at Master Chia's excellent *'Universal Healing Tao'* web site: www.universal-tao.com.

1. Sit comfortably and begin to focus on balanced breathing until you are breathing gently, smoothly, deeply, evenly, calmly and softly. Relax your forehead, let your eyes, ears and tongue soften. Allow your face to become relaxed and calm.

2. Imagine yourself in one of your favorite, most beautiful places in the world surrounded by the beauty and vitality of nature. Begin to smile, and as you experience the joy and happiness of your favorite place, amplify your smile, feel it in your face, your mouth, your eyes.

3. Let your relaxed smiling awareness flow down through your cheeks, down through your jaw muscles and tongue, and down through your neck and throat, soothing and calming as it goes.

4. Smile down to your chest and into your heart. Sense them opening like a flower with love, joy and happiness bubbling out of them. Do balanced breathing of the love and joy from your heart into your smile and into the saliva in your mouth.

5. Roll your tongue around your mouth until you have gathered a nice amount of saliva. Smile to the saliva and draw the smiling energy and golden light into the saliva transforming it into delicious healing nectar. Really feel this. Really taste the golden sweet smile into your saliva.

6. Swallow the saliva in two or three easy positive swallows. Follow it with awareness down your esophagus, smiling as it goes, feeling the healing nectar soothing and refreshing your esophagus.

7. Continue smiling through the rest of your digestive tract: your stomach, small intestine, gall bladder, large intestine, rectum, bladder and urethra. Thank these organs for their work in giving you energy through the processes they do.

8. Return your awareness once more to your smile and your eyes and recharge your smiling energy, directing it all around you here in one of your favorite, most beautiful places in your world.

9. Return to the here and now, filled in heart, mind, body and soul with your inner smile — filled with the joy of life deep within you now.

Notes/Thoughts/Insights:

Congruence

Now it's time for you to put your learnings into action by facilitating congruence between your three brains with the *m*BIT Foundational Sequence. In this discovery exercise you'll first get into a coherent state via balanced breathing. You'll then explore integrating your three brains' different core competencies starting with your heart brain, then up to your head brain, back down through the heart and into your gut brain, finally ending back at the heart.

While this discovery exercise works with the core competencies of passion (heart), curiosity (head), and motivated action (gut), you can modify this exercise to integrate any of the balanced states listed in the *m*BIT Core Competencies Framework.

1. Think of an issue or situation in which you would like to embody more passion and take more motivated action.

2. Now sit or stand comfortably and begin Balanced Breathing.

3. Once you have balanced your breathing for a few minutes along the sine wave pattern (breathing in for 6 seconds and out for 6 seconds), begin to recall a memory or imagine a scenario that produces a strong feeling of passion within you. This could involve engaging in activities you love to do, loved to do in the past, or would love to do in the future or as an aspiration. Connect strongly with these feelings of passion that arise within you as you do this.

4. As you fully experience your feelings of passion, breathe into your heart area and feel the feelings of passion filling your chest and heart with each breath. Amplify these feelings at least ten times for a deep, rich, heart-full experience.

5. Now begin to imagine and feel your feelings of passion expanding upwards to your head brain. As you send the signals of passion upward, allow your head to become filled with curiosity. Become curious about this passion. Entertain curious thoughts and perceptions about the nature of your passionate feelings, discover different possibilities for expressing your feeling of passion, and explore new ways

229

of seeing and understanding the world starting from intense feelings of passion. Be open to what is there to learn with all of this and amplify your curiosity by ten times more.

6. Now begin to breathe this passionate curiosity from your head back down into your heart. Feel the thoughts of curiosity harmonize with and enhance your feelings of passion.

7. Now continue to balanced breathe the feelings of passion from your heart combined with the curiosity of your head down into your gut area. Feel the sensations and impulse signals of your gut intelligence instinctively moving toward taking some kind of positive action from your combination of passion and curiosity. Let this feeling of motivated action fill your entire lower abdomen, hips and legs. Amplify your feeling of motivated action by ten times or more.

8. Now breathe these feelings and sensations of motivated action back up into your heart. As you send these signals upwards, allow each balanced breath to help you feel more and more strongly the integration and growing congruence between the passionate feelings of your heart, the curious thoughts and perceptions of your head, and the impulse to take motivated actions from your gut. Expand that flow throughout your entire body and notice the changes in your overall wellbeing with your enhanced and expanded sense of who you are and what is truly possible for you now.

Notes/Thoughts/Insights:

Utilizing NIE's (Neural Integrative Engagements)

In this exercise you'll perform the *m*BIT Foundational Sequence adding in various NIE's to facilitate increased levels of engagement with each neural network.

There are many ways to work with NIE's and the following is just a starting point to begin exploring and experimenting with them. You'll want to play with a range of variations and combinations to find the specific NIE's that work best for you in particular situations.

1. Think of an issue or situation in which you'd like to experience a deeper connection with a core value and being able to express it congruently in your behaviors. Identify a specific issue or situation, and identify the specific core value. Examples of core values include joy, peace, happiness, love, integrity, respect, gratitude, honesty, etc.

2. Sit or stand comfortably and begin Balanced Breathing.

3. Once you have balanced your breathing for a few minutes along the wave pattern (breathing in for 6 seconds and out for 6 seconds), begin to visualize an image that best represents your core value to you. Allow your unconscious mind to '*intuitively*' arrive at an appropriate image for you.

4. Explore making the image in your mind bigger, brighter and more colorful. Bring it closer toward you and notice how your feelings and sensations change. Make refined adjustments to your image until it produces a strong feeling within you.

5. Now imagine a color for your core value. Imagine that color totally surrounding you like a comforting blanket. Breathe in that color. Breathe it into your lungs and allow the color to fill your heart area. Feel your value coming more and more alive in your heart as you breathe its color into you.

6. Feel the sensations associated with your core value moving through you and expanding your chest area with each breath. Feel its temperature and allow its

movement to begin to rise up toward your head. You may even hear some sounds or tones as the sensations of your core value rises up and reaches your head.

7. See and feel your head fill with the color of your core value and allow it to color all of your thoughts, perceptions and internal dialogue. Hear how your own internal voice changes when speaking from the essence of your core value. Notice the new ways of thinking and new perceptions available to you now about your situation or issue.

8. Now imagine your core value flowing down from your head back down to your heart as easily as water flows downward along the natural contours of a terrain. Feel your heart fill with new ways of relating to others and to your specific situation or issue based on living and breathing your core value.

9. Now continue to allow the enhanced feelings and new perceptions from your core value to flow down to your gut area. Feel it gather there like a pool of living energy. Feel the pulse of life and your own aliveness. Feel yourself awakening and moving with the pulse of your core value. Feel the impulse to move and act in accordance with the energy and truth of your core value. Be aware of the behavioral choices becoming available to you that embody, express and fulfill your core value into the physical world. Make a subtle or clear movement, gesture or stance that symbolizes to you the beginnings of a physical/behavioral manifestation of your core value.

10. Now take a deep breath and feel the energy of your core value begin to rise like an *'aliveness thermometer'* until it again reaches your heart. Breathe in the energy, colors, and sounds of your core value. Let it fill your heart as you gently sway and move to the pulse and rhythm of your core value. Imagine the fragrance your core value filling your nostrils and evoking new possibilities for experiencing your situation or issue. Imagine the taste of your core value as you gently swallow it into you, making it part of your very being.

11. Allow your core value to flow easily throughout your entire body and notice the changes in your overall wellbeing. Become aware of your enhanced and expanded sense of who you are and how you can now act in ways that express your authentic self.

Notes/Thoughts/Insights:

Compassionate Self Connection

You cannot truly understand compassion by intellectualizing it from your head brain. You won't '*get it*' since its main home is in the heart. It's more than just an emotional feeling state, it's a state of being. While compassion is expressed through the heart intelligence it arises from a state of highly coherent integration between all three brains. Compassion is a natural expression of the fully integrated '*You*' as a conscious human being, aware of your inter-connectedness with all other living beings.

In the following exercise, you'll learn to experience compassion as a Highest Expression of your self.

Connecting to how you currently relate to yourself

1. Sit comfortably and allow yourself to settle into your body. Breathe deeply, slowly, gently and comfortably. Calm and settle your mind enough that you can tune into yourself and be aware of your internal experience. You may wish to close your eyes if that helps you focus inward.

2. Begin to become aware of your relationship with yourself. As you think about yourself, who you are as a person, your strengths and weaknesses, what you've done and not done in life, start to scan each of your brains for their responses. Become aware of how you feel about yourself and the emotional quality of how you relate to yourself. Notice your head brain's internal dialogue and what it's saying about yourself. Notice the language and tone of voice it uses. Be aware of your own gut response to yourself. How is your gut reacting and relating to who you are?

3. Now stand up and shake your body a little to shift out of this state. Sit back down in readiness to enter a state of compassion.

Connecting to Compassion

4. Sitting comfortably, do Balanced Breathing for a few minutes until you are in a balanced coherent state.

5. Begin to breathe compassion and loving-kindness into your heart and chest area. Feel the feelings of compassion flow in and out of your heart and chest area with each breath. See the color of compassion (whatever that is for you) flowing in and out of you with each breath. Surround yourself with this color until you are bathed in it. Hear the sound(s) of compassion (whatever they may be for you) at just the right volume so that you experience it vibrantly in and throughout your body.

6. Now expand the feelings of compassion from your heart area until they fill your entire body. Intensify and expand these feelings even further until you are being compassion itself. Notice the changes in your gut brain as you become compassion. Notice how the thoughts, perceptions and internal dialogue change as you become the very essence of compassion and loving-kindness. Continue to be aware of the changes in your gut brain as you become the embodiment of compassion itself. Start to exude compassion outwards from yourself so that you feel a strong desire to reach out, connect, and to help.

Extending Compassion to Yourself

7. While '*being*' and exuding strong feelings of compassion, begin to think of yourself. Relate to yourself from a consciousness of compassion and loving-kindness. See yourself as someone who is intrinsically good, doing the best they can with what they know and don't know. Appreciate yourself as someone who has come this far given your personal history, upbringing and life conditions. Have compassion for how you've had to deal with your challenges, struggles and conditioning. Appreciate and celebrate your strengths, abilities, passions, joyful moments and personal victories in life. Give yourself the gift of understanding, the grace of acceptance and non-judgment, and the freedom to be who you are.

8. From this state of appreciating and affirming yourself, become aware of how your sense of self — who you truly are at a deep level and your intrinsic worth — is expanding and evolving. As you feel more positively connected with yourself,

notice what new possibilities become available for you in how you can authentically express your truest self in your daily life.

Notes/Thoughts/Insights:

Compassion for Others

In this exercise, you'll learn to experience compassion for others as a Highest Expression.

1. Identity someone with whom you would like to show more compassion. Often, your indicators are in the form of incongruency signals; tensions or conflicts within you because there's a part of you thinking, feeling and behaving in a non-compassionate way toward that person. Or there's some part of you that says you should be more understanding, kinder, or gracious. These feelings of incongruency are signals of in-authenticity, where your ego is reacting in one way and a deeper, more authentic self knows those reactions are not representative of who you truly are at your Highest Expression of self.

Connecting to how you currently relate to other person

2. Sit comfortably and allow yourself to settle into your body. Breathe deeply, slowly, gently and comfortably. Settle your mind enough that you can tune into yourself and be aware of your internal experience. You may wish to close your eyes if that helps you focus inward.

3. Begin to become aware of your relationship with this other person. As you think about this person and whatever it is they may have done or didn't do, notice your reactions in your gut, heart and head.

4. As you notice your reactions, become aware of how you feel about yourself when you react this way. Do you like yourself when you react this way? Do you respect yourself when you react this way? Notice the differences between what your ego defenses come up with versus what a truer, deeper, and more authentic '*you*' says and feels.

5. Now stand up and shake your body a little to shift out of this state. Sit back down in readiness to enter a state of compassion.

Connecting to Compassion

6. Sitting comfortably, do Balanced Breathing for a few minutes until you are in a deeply balanced and coherent state.

7. Begin to breathe compassion and loving-kindness into your heart and chest area. Feel the feelings of compassion flow in and out of your heart and chest area with each breath. See the color of compassion (whatever that is for you) flowing in and out of your heart region with each breath. Surround yourself with your color until you are bathed in it. Hear the sound(s) of compassion (whatever they may be for you) at just the right volume so that you experience it vibrantly in and throughout your body.

8. Now expand your feelings of compassion from your heart area up into your head and then down into your gut until they fill your entire body. Intensify and expand the feelings even further until you are being compassion itself. Notice the changes in your gut brain as YOU become compassion. Notice how the thoughts, perceptions and internal dialogue change as YOU become the very essence of compassion. Continue to be aware of the changes in your gut brain as YOU become the embodiment of compassion itself. Start to exude compassion outwards from yourself so that you feel a strong desire to reach out, connect, and to help.

Extending Compassion to the Other Person

9. While experiencing, being and exuding strong feelings of deep compassion, forgiveness and loving-kindness, begin to think of the other person. Relate to the other person from a consciousness of compassion. See them not as their behaviors but as a person, a human being, someone who is intrinsically good, doing the best they can with what they know and don't know. Appreciate them as someone who has a come through a personal history and upbringing, much of which you probably don't know about. Even if you do, you haven't lived their life through their struggles, insecurities, fears, challenges and triumphs. Can you honestly judge them from inside your skin, not being them? Have compassion for how

they've had to deal with their challenges, struggles and conditioning. Recognize, acknowledge and appreciate the strengths they must have in order to have made it to where they've gotten to so far. Give them the gift of your understanding, the grace of your acceptance and non-judgment, and the freedom to be who they are, not as you want them to be. Be open to how you can relate to them differently now in your attitude, behaviors, and speech.

10. From this state of appreciating and affirming their innate worth as a human being, become aware of how your sense of self — who you truly are at a deep level and your own intrinsic worth — is expanding and evolving. Notice how, as you connect compassionately with others, you feel more positively connected with yourself, a more authentic '*you*'. Notice what new possibilities become available for how you can authentically express your truest self in your daily life.

Notes/Thoughts/Insights:

Embodying Courage

Preparation

1. Sit comfortably and allow yourself to settle into your body. Breathe deeply, slowly, gently and comfortably. Settle your mind enough that you can tune into yourself and be aware of your internal experience. You may wish to close your eyes if that helps you focus inward.

2. Think of a situation where you'd like to embody more gutsy courage in order to more fully express who you truly are at a deep level. There may be situations in which fear, anxiety, insecurity, worry, self-doubt, or a lack of self-belief prevents you from taking action on your dreams, passions, goals, aspirations, beliefs and convictions, or living your values.

3. Now stand up and shake your body a little to shift out of this state. Sit back down in readiness to enter a state of courageous expression.

Connecting to Courage (starting with the heart, then engaging the gut)

4. Sitting comfortably, do Balanced Breathing for a few minutes until you are in a deeply balanced and coherent state.

5. Begin to connect with the values that are important to you and you want to express in this situation. Imagine having the courage to act on these values, and breathe that courage into your heart and chest area. Feel the feelings of courage flow in and out of your heart and chest area with each breath. It can help to imagine images of courageous people doing gutsy, brave and courageous acts from movies, books or real life. Or you may wish to hear in your mind some music or soundtracks that inspires you to strongly courageous action. See the color of courage (whatever that is for you) flowing in and out of you with each breath. Hear the sound(s) of courage (whatever that may be for you) at just the right volume so that your heart is filled with courage.

6. Notice what values and deep feelings arise within you that remind you of the personal importance of acting in this situation despite your fears and insecurities. Connect deeply with these values and powerful feelings, and expand them so that you experience them as BIG, bold, strong, deep, and powerful.

7. Now breathe these powerful feelings down into your gut. Feel the feelings connect with your gut to produce the sensations of courage for action. Feel the strength and power of your values overriding the sensations of fear, insecurity, and anxiety. Feel your courage build within you, expanding into and filling your gut, your entire lower abdomen, your pelvis and hips, and extending down into your legs. Feel yourself want to physically move and take action.

8. Breathe the color(s) and sound(s) of courage (whatever that is for you) into your gut area and lower torso. Surround yourself with these colors and sounds until you are bathed in them and so that you experience them intensely in and throughout your body. Intensify and expand the feelings even further until you are being courage itself. Notice the changes in your gut brain as YOU become courage. En-couraged by your heart, notice how your thoughts, perceptions and internal dialogue change as YOU become the very essence of courage.

Acting from Courage

9. While feeling and being courageous, think of the situation you want to act on. See yourself in your mind's eye taking courageous action, expressing your deepest values of who you are as a person. Imagine the feelings of taking action, en-couraged and motivated by your heart, mobilized by your gut. Allow your head brain to create several options for how you might be able to take a range of different actions so that whatever you do fully expresses who you are as well as optimizes the impacts you generate and create for positive results.

10. From this state of '*being*' courage, become aware of how your sense of self — who you truly are at the deepest levels and your intrinsic worth — is expanding and evolving. As you feel more positively connected within yourself, notice what new

possibilities become available for you in how you can authentically express your truest self in your daily life.

Notes/Thoughts/Insights:

Integrating Creativity

Preparation

1. Sit comfortably and allow yourself to settle into your body. Breathe deeply, slowly, gently and comfortably. Settle your mind enough that you can tune into yourself and be aware of your internal experience. You may wish to close your eyes if that helps you focus inward.

2. Think of a situation in which you feel stuck, limited, or would like more choices in how to respond.

3. Sitting comfortably, do Balanced Breathing for a few minutes until you are in a deeply balanced and coherent state.

Connecting to Creativity

4. Become aware of what values are important for you to express in this situation. Allow those values to come alive and experience them deeply in your heart. Breathe those values into your heart.

5. Now imagine yourself having the creativity to be able to express those values through a wide range of behaviors and responses. You don't have to know what those behaviors and responses actually are yet, you only need to connect with the idea of being creative enough to generate them. You may find it helpful to imagine images of creative people from movies, books or real life as role models. Or you might find it helpful to imagine creative works that inspire you and fill you with a sense of creativity. Allow your heart to value this creativity and fully appreciate its importance and worth in expressing your truest self.

6. Begin to breathe creativity into your heart and chest area. Feel the feelings of creativity flow in and out of your heart and chest area with each breath. See the color of creativity (whatever that is for you) flowing in and out of you with each

breath. Surround yourself with this color until you are bathed deeply in it. Hear the sound(s) of creativity (whatever that may be for you) at just the right volume so that you experience it vibrantly in and throughout your body.

Generating Creative Options

7. Now breathe your creativity up into your head brain. Feel your head become filled with creativity. Feel it expand and extend to your face, your neck, and your shoulders. Notice the free-form flow of thoughts, images, and sounds that arise within your head brain. Notice and appreciate how easily your head brain creates and comes up with whatever it does without you even having to try.

8. While continuing your Balanced Breathing, ask your head brain to imagine at least three new options for how you might respond to your situation in ways that fulfill the value(s) you want to express here. Don't try to analyze or consciously figure out these options. Simply keep focusing on your balanced breathing, feel the desired value(s) in your heart and allow those feelings to flow up into your head, hold your intention to create new options, and allow your head brain to freely generate these options for you. Just observe your thoughts, images, and internal narrative as they arise. Allow the new options to emerge and form on their own as you hold your intention to bring them forth into a clear creative and generative pattern.

9. As each new option emerges, do not judge it or evaluate it, especially not by the criteria of your current thinking. Simply thank all three of your brains for working together and generating new creative options, and just receive them. Each option may or may not be fully formed. You are purely after the creation of new options for thinking about the situation and how to approach it differently. Also, your head brain may generate more than just the three options originally requested. Be open to all creative possibilities.

Creative Alignment and Integration

10. Once an option has emerged that you resonate with, bring that option down into your heart. Allow your heart to value it and bring emotional significance to it. The specifics of the new options may start to modify in accordance with the heart's '*e-value-ation*'.

11. Now breathe that '*re-e-value-ated*' option down into your gut area. Allow your gut intelligence to assimilate and modify that option even further so that you feel you can and want to congruently and intuitively act on that option. Feel how the option is transformed by your wise and intuitive gut intelligence so that taking action is now a natural expression of who you are and a natural expression of you manifesting your highest intention into your world.

12. Now breathe your transformed option back up into your heart, re-value that option in its new form, and from this state of appreciating the value of creativity and yourself as an inherently creative person, become aware of how your sense of self is expanding and evolving. As you feel more positively connected with yourself, notice what new possibilities become available for you in how you can authentically express your truest self in your daily life.

Notes/Thoughts/Insights:

Highest Expressions

1. Think of an issue or situation in which you would like to embody a way of being that is more connected and congruent with your sense of whom you truly are; your authentic self. This may be an issue or situation where you are or have been behaving in a way that's reactive, ego-driven, defensive, or fearful. You can recognize it because your experience is of some form of suffering. Deep down you know you shouldn't or don't really want to behave in the way you have been. Deep down, you know that your behaviors are reactive and they don't really represent who you really are.

2. Now sit or stand comfortably and begin Balanced Breathing.

3. Once you have balanced your breathing for a few minutes along the wave pattern (breathing in for 6 seconds and out for 6 seconds), begin to recall a memory or imagine a scenario that produces strong feelings of compassion within you. Utilize NIE's such as visualizing the color of compassion and breathing it in, imagining the sound of compassion and letting it fill your heart, etc. Connect strongly with the feelings of compassion and loving-kindness that arise within you as you do this.

4. As you fully experience these feelings of compassion, breathe into your heart area and feel the feelings of compassion filling your chest and heart with each breath. Allow the feelings of compassion to resonate deeply with your sense of who you are at an authentic, essence level. Amplify the feelings at least ten times now for a deep, rich, heart-full experience of yourself with a consciousness of compassion.

5. Now begin to imagine and feel the feelings of '*you*' as a compassionate self, expanding upwards to your head brain. As you send the signals of compassion upward, allow your head brain to become filled with compassion and creativity. Connect with the realization that you are a creative being. Starting from a consciousness of compassion, experience your innate and natural creative abilities

going to work and beginning to imagine new ways of being and responding to your issue/situation. Observe and enjoy how your head brain easily produces more and more new ways to compassionately and creatively respond to your issue/situation.

6. Now begin to breathe these feelings of you being a compassionate and creative self, from your head back down into your heart. Allow your heart the freedom to appreciate and value the various options and new responses generated by your creative head brain. Let your compassionate heart prioritize the value of these new choices based on their resonance with the essence of who you truly are as a self-aware human being.

7. Now continue to breathe the feelings of creative compassion and these new choices down into your gut brain. Feel your gut brain assimilate the most congruent and resonant choices into your very being. Feel the naturally arising impulse to act courageously on the most resonant choices, as a natural expression of who you truly are as a compassionate, creative and courageous person. Feel the resonance of acting in accordance with who you truly are as a conscious, self aware human being. Amplify this feeling of courageous action by ten times or more!

8. Now breathe these compassionate, creative and courageous feelings back up into your heart. As these signals naturally and easily flow upwards, become more and more aware of your authentic sense of self, of who you truly are at a deep level of essence, resonating deeply with your expressive nature of compassion, creativity and courage. Be open to and aware of the changes in your overall wellbeing and your expanded sense of who you really, truly are and how you can express your integrated authentic self into the world now.

Notes/Thoughts/Insights:

Intuition

In this exercise you'll learn to gain insights and deeply intuitive messages from your unconscious mind and multiple brains.

1. Think of an issue or situation in which you'd like to tap into your intuition and inner wisdom.

2. Now sit comfortably in a quiet room, free from interruptions or distractions and begin Highest Expression Balanced Breathing.

3. Inner stillness is a pre-requisite to tapping into intuition, so make sure you guide yourself into a deeply calm and peaceful state of coherence. Align your heart, head and gut brains by breathing in peace, joy and compassion and moving these feelings and messages across your three brains.

4. Once you are calmly aligned, respectfully ask yourself questions about your situation and listen to the first answers that pop into your mind. They might be images, sounds, a felt-sense, feelings or some words. Whatever they are, just notice them. Pay attention. Thank your brains for the messages. Now begin to explore what they mean. Ask your unconscious mind to help you understand their insights. Don't force this, just allow the intuitions and ideas to flow naturally into your conscious awareness. You can ask each of your brains individually for their wisdom. Ask your heart what it means. Ask your gut. Ask your head. And keep Balanced Breathing as you do and continue calm Balanced Breathing as you wait for their responses.

5. Remember that intuition is calm and not fearful. So if you feel any strongly visceral fear or panic based response then note it and Balanced Breathe until you come back to autonomic coherence. Then ask your brains to tell you what is driving the response, what is the intuition or insight you need to learn in order to bring generative wisdom to your situation. This is all about unpacking the deeper messages that underlay the initial response.

6. With trust, respect and practice you'll find that your deep intuitions become more accurate, more insightful and come to conscious awareness more quickly and with greater ease.

Notes/Thoughts/Insights:

Calm Abiding 'In joy in yourself'

In this exercise you'll build a deep state of calm peaceful joy within your heart, head and gut.

1. Whenever you're feeling stressed or in need of some uplifting or calming, simply take a few minutes to sit and start Balanced Breathing. Breathe in and out calmly and evenly, taking approx. 6 seconds on the in-breath and 6 seconds on the out-breath. As you know, make sure your in and out breaths are of the same duration.

2. As you breathe in, imagine that each breath is uplifting your heart with light-hearted joy. Really feel that uplifting feeling. And smile as you do this. Smiling makes a key difference. Deeply feel your heart being uplifted as you breathe. You can imagine a color or sparkling light filling your heart with uplifting positive energy and love. And you can take that light, color and feeling and experience it going all the way from your heart to your head, taking your delightful, joyful and uplifting feelings and messages from your heart into your mind.

3. As you breathe out, imagine your breath going down from your head/heart to your gut, taking with it calming feelings and messages. Really feel that letting go, relaxing, calming and peace-filled sense of joy fill your belly. Add a light or color that deeply enhances your gut-felt feelings of peace, joy and contentment.

4. Breathe in '*uplifting in-joy-in your heart*', breath out and down '*deeply calming in-joy-in your gut*'. Continue doing this, as you smile, swallowing peaceful joy from your head to your gut and feeling so profoundly aligned, peacefully integrated and joyfully calmed.

Notes/Thoughts/Insights:

Deep Inner Forgiving

When doing forgiving, it's important to realize you cannot easily get to highly coherent states of loving-kindness and forgiveness when you are in overly sympathetic or parasympathetic modes of functioning. You must first get yourself into a state of coherence, generate pure states of love and forgiveness and then apply those states to whom or what you want to forgive.

1. Identify with whom or with what you want to do '*forgiving*'.

2. Sit comfortably and engage in Balanced Breathing for several minutes.

3. Set aside for now any and all of your current feelings of '*unforgiveness*' (e.g. anger, resentment, hurt, being offended, violation, betrayal, etc.). Regardless of what happened and your internal dialogue about it, focus on maintaining your Balanced Breathing. Create a clear mental and emotional '*space*' within you to access feelings of forgiveness and love as pure states, not associated (yet) with your memories of who or whatever happened.

4. With each breath, create and hold feelings of pure forgiving and loving in your heart. As you breathe in and out, amplify the feelings with each breath, feel them expand and grow, until your whole chest, your whole torso, your whole body is filled with deep feelings of loving-kindness. Make sure you expand them from your heart to your head and then back through the heart down deeply to your gut, deep inside your torso and stomach. This will send important messages from your heart brain to your head and gut brains. This will align your three brains together around deep and total forgiveness. Keep expanding these pure feelings of forgiving and loving until they fill your entire body and way of being.

5. Now start to think of who or what you want to forgive. Continue to breathe and amplify your heart, head and gut feelings of forgiveness and compassion as you think of who or what you are forgiving. Breathe forgiveness and compassion into your head brain and notice how your thoughts, perceptions and meaning of what

happened begins to change and soften. Notice your openness to new ways of understanding the person or situation from a place of compassion, loving-kindness, and a generosity of spirit.

6. Breathe these new understandings and new awareness back down into your heart. Value these new perceptions highly. Notice how forgiving feels good, how it brings greater peace and wellness to you. Be aware of how your heart opens and lightens up.

7. Now breathe these enhanced and highly valued feelings and perceptions down into your gut. Swallow them down if that helps. Feel your gut take in and assimilate these new learnings. Feel your gut relax and '*let go*' of any tensions related to defensiveness, protection, or aggression. Feel how your gut welcomes and responds with a sense of ease, peace and security. As your gut lets go of the old way of being, feel how it and you are becoming increasingly ready to move on in life. Feel how letting go of this past '*baggage*' makes you feel lighter, freer, and makes it easier to focus on moving forward from now on in. Experience the sensations of your gut updating its learned responses, releasing what is no longer useful to hold onto, and mobilizing you toward acting from a new, freer identity.

8. If you experience any Neural Integration Blocks (NIB's) during any part of this process, talk to your *m*BIT Coach and get them to help you dissolve and pattern-interrupt those NIB's and then return to Step 4 above and re-do the steps of the exercise till you can experience deep integrated forgiving.

9. Say to yourself:

   "I forgive. I do forgiving, I feel forgiving, I am forgiving. I forgive [*the name of who or what you have forgiven*] completely. I release any and all un-useful feelings and stories that do not serve me and that do not express my truest self. I forgive myself completely. I am a worthwhile person who deserves loving-kindness and support. I let go and am now ready to move on in my life."

Say these words several times, with warm, loving tonalities. Hug yourself both physically and in your imagination. And all the while keep breathing love and forgiveness into your heart, your head and your gut.

You may wish to repeat this process two or three times. Each time you practice the '*doing*' of forgiving and compassion you'll find it gets stronger, easier and more integrated into your evolving sense of self. Your heart and gut brains will learn and remember how to do this re-patterning process more easily and quickly with any other people or issues you need to or want to forgive.

Notes/Thoughts/Insights:

mBrain Mindfulness Meditation

In this exercise you'll learn to calmly direct your attention towards what's happening in your mind, body and multiple brains.

1. Start in a comfortable sitting position. This is an eyes-open exercise and is best done in a relatively quiet environment. Sit so that your posture is upright and not rigid. Allow your spine to gently straighten, keep your head nicely balanced, your feet flat on the floor and your hands resting comfortably in your lap. Set your gaze so that it softly and easily focuses on the floor somewhere in front of you.

2. Commence Balanced Breathing along the sine wave pattern so that you are breathing in for 6 seconds and out for 6 seconds, evenly and effortlessly. Do this for a couple of minutes till you can feel the calm experience of coherence envelop your heart, head and gut brains.

3. Put aside any thoughts of the past or future and stay focused in the present. Keep your attention on your Balanced Breathing, noticing the air moving in and out of your lungs, feeling the rise and fall of your belly and diaphragm. Focus on how each breath is new and fresh. Allow your breathing to continue naturally, without being controlled.

4. Start to watch and experience any thoughts, feelings or sensations as they arise. Notice where in your body they begin and move to and from. Are they from and in your heart? Are they from and in your gut? Are they head based? Don't ignore any thoughts or feelings and don't suppress them either. Just simply observe them and remain calm as you continue to breathe in a balanced and coherent way.

5. Your goal with this exercise is to stay present and gain insight into your experience of reality. Your intention is to be mindful and aware of what's happening within your mind, body and multiple brains. Simply sitting, breathing and noticing your ongoing internal experience. Everything is welcomed. Nothing is ignored.

Similarly nothing is analyzed. Just notice the patterns of your thoughts, feelings and messages that are flowing in your mind and body.

6. There is no failure with this exercise. If you notice your attention wandering, then gently and calmly bring it back to your breathing. If you find yourself lost in discursive thought, in confusion or in analysis, just calmly bring your focus back to your breathing. The act of noticing is itself part of mindfulness. Your role is to play the part of an impartial observer of your ongoing attention and experience.

7. When you have performed the exercise for the allotted period of 10 or more minutes, finish by breathing compassion into your heart, move that up to your head where you can add creativity and then breath both of them back through your heart to your gut, adding in gutsy courage to your experience. Cycle through your Highest Expressions across several breaths, building up the wonderful and generative experience that they bring. Finally, stand up slowly and gently stretch, feeling alive, energized and renewed.

The aim of mindfulness meditation is to achieve a mind that is stable, aware and calm. Through mindfulness practice you develop and strengthen your neural circuits in the skills of peace, calmness and emergent wisdom. The more often you practice the greater the results. Even 10 minutes a day can make a world of difference to how your brains calmly integrate and communicate together to produce generative awareness in your life.

Notes/Thoughts/Insights:

Hungering for Success

In this exercise you'll build a deep visceral hunger in your gut for an intensely heart-felt goal or outcome. This exercise is about building intense motivation, a deep sense of encouragement and a passionate and congruent hunger for the success of your outcome. [Note: do NOT do this exercise immediately after a meal, it is better done when you are physically hungry.]

1. Think of an outcome, goal or dream that you want to have achieved. Make sure it is well-formed, achievable and ecological in your life. For example, there must be no negative consequences for yourself or others. It should also be self-initiated and achievable within your control. And there must be specific steps and tasks that you can begin immediately so that you are moving towards your outcome in a relatively expedient timeframe.

2. Begin Balanced Breathing for a couple of minutes until you are in a deeply coherent and balanced state.

3. Start connecting to the values and intentions that underpin your outcome and feel these deeply in your heart. Breathe your passion and desire for your outcome into your heart. Expand these feelings throughout your chest region and breathe them up into your head and down into your gut. Add in colors, sparkle, sounds, images, whatever adds to and enhances your experience of your outcome and its connected values.

4. As you are breathing your values, desires and a passionate sense of your outcome down into your gut, begin to feel a real and growing hunger for your outcome. Imagine that you can almost taste your outcome and it's delicious. Savor it. Salivate for it. Massively desire it! Intensify your hunger for it. Really build an incredible taste and hunger in your gut for your outcome. And cycle with your breathing from feeling the passion and desire for your outcome in your heart,

down to an incredible hunger for achieving your outcome in your gut. Intensely feel the motivation to start moving on making your outcome a reality now.

5. Once you have cycled between your gut and heart a number of times, amplifying it with every pass, begin to add in your head-based creativity. Move the sense of your outcome up into your head and focus on allowing your unconscious mind to generate creative ways to help you get moving on your goals and ways to quickly and powerfully achieve the results you so hungrily desire.

6. With each option that your head brain brings forth, cycle through steps 4 and 5 and feel yourself getting more and more motivated and excited to take action NOW!

Notes/Thoughts/Insights:

Pushing through Fear

In this exercise you'll practice creatively using your head and heart to motivate your gut to push through gut-felt feelings of fear. While it's best to practice this ahead of time in safe and comfortable situations, it can be used in acute situations where you need to overcome debilitating fear. The more you practice this, the more the process will become available to you in the heat of the moment in which it is needed.

[**Important Note:** This exercise is NOT to be used with phobias or other intense psychological or emotional abreactions. You should seek professional guidance when working with such issues. This exercise also doesn't address issues of chronic anxiety. It is designed for pushing through normal, situationally-based immediate fear where taking action is an appropriate response.]

1. Think of an issue or situation in which you experience fear that prevents you from taking appropriate and necessary action, and that you need to push through. Start remembering or thinking of the situation vividly enough that you feel the sensations related to the fear.

2. It is massively important in such situations that you immediately begin Balanced Breathing to control your autonomic balance. You'll find that in fear filled situations, your breathing will NOT be balanced, and so it's vital you control this consciously. Balanced breathe for a number of minutes until you are in a coherent and balanced state.

3. The next step begins in your head. Notice the fear sensations occurring in your gut and body. Talk to yourself and label these sensations. Become aware of how your true identity, who you are in your Highest Expression of self, is separate from these sensations. Notice that there is a '*you*' that can actually observe them. Notice also how you are bigger and better than these sensations and mere reactions, and in spite of these, you can choose to respond more generatively. Tell yourself what

you want to and have to do in this situation that is truly representative of what's deeply important to you and who you know yourself to truly be.

4. Balanced Breathe your ideal sense of self and the values that truly define you from your head down to your heart. Feel them so very strongly and deeply in your heart. Brighten them up. Add in the color of your deepest and truest sense of self. Expand these in your heart. Amplify them with every breath. Tell yourself as you breathe down into your heart what you must do, what you have to do, what you can't NOT do! Link this sense of truth deeply into your heart.

5. And when you are ready, take a big breath in and send this deep conviction down to the back of your gut! Swallow hard. Zoom your conviction and determination into your gut. Really feel it pack a punch! Straighten up your entire spine all the way down from your lower back and pelvis. Really feel your gutsy determination slot powerfully in. And as it hits the back of your gut, make a deep guttural sound and move forward. Actually step forward. Fast! And grunt, growl, or yell a powerful sound out loud. Like a powerful martial artist in action! Physically move as you make these sounds and push through that fear. Push forward into the true embodied action of your highest self. You can do it! You cannot NOT do it! You are powerful, bold and filled with courage!

6. Feel powerfully and massively emboldened with your new found courage to act in spite of the mere sensations of fear and TAKE ACTION NOW!

Notes/Thoughts/Insights:

Dissolving Compulsive Urges

In this exercise you'll practice using your heart, head and gut to align, forgive, accept and satiate compulsive urges.

1. Do this exercise when you're feeling any compulsive urges that you want to interrupt and dissolve. Begin by calmly accepting your situation, your feelings and the current experience of the compulsion.

2. If you can, sit in a comfortable balanced position. Allow your spine to gently straighten, keep your head nicely balanced, your feet flat on the floor and your hands resting comfortably in your lap. Set your gaze so that it softly and easily focuses on the floor somewhere in front of you.

3. Commence Balanced Breathing along the sine wave pattern so that you're breathing in for 6 seconds and out for 6 seconds, evenly and effortlessly. Do this for a couple of minutes till you can feel the calm experience of coherence deeply envelop your heart, head and gut brains.

4. With your right hand, gently touch your heart region and remind yourself that you are worthy of love. As you do this, begin to breathe love, compassion and a positive feeling of appreciation into your heart. With every breath expand and intensify your feelings of loving-kindness and compassion throughout your chest and up into your head, and then down deep into your gut. Enhance this with colors and sounds. As you move your feelings from your heart to your head, add in creativity, and then as you move those feelings back to your heart and then to your gut, add in deep feelings of gutsy courage. Flow these wonderful integrated feelings of love, kindness, compassion, creativity and courage up and down and throughout your mind and body.

5. As you think about those compulsive feelings you were having, become curious about them. See those old compulsive urges as a gift of information. Ask each of your multiple brains, "What do I really need?", "What message was the

compulsive feeling giving me that I need to acknowledge?" and "What are the intentions of that compulsion?" Listen to your intuitive answers, responses and feelings from each of your brains. Thank the gift of your compulsion for bringing powerful insights to your life, so that you can now begin to creatively find ways to honor the intentions and needs that underlay those old compulsive urges. Thank the parts of your multiple brains that were doing the compulsing in their best efforts to support and protect you.

6. Continue your Balanced Breathing from your Highest Expressions, and ask your creative head brain to come up with at least three new ways to better honor those messages and intentions that underlay the old compulsive urges. Be sure your heart and gut brains are supporting the head brain by being involved in generating these new options.

7. Now take your sense of each creative and generative solution and breathe it from your head down deeply into your heart, really feel it merge with your love and compassion. Then when you are ready, swallow your creative positive new behavior and solution deeply into your gut. Feel it satiate the old compulsion. Feel your gut fill with love, forgiveness, support and calm, peaceful joy. Really taste those feelings and swallow them down into your gut. Let the experience of joy and appreciation for yourself and your life fill your stomach, fill your torso, fill your gut brain and fill your body all the way back up to your heart and beyond. Finish by feeling an incredible sense of value, appreciation and love in your heart, mind and soul for your wonderful life and your wonderful generative self as you move forward in life.

8. As you do this exercise, if you experience any major Neural Integration Blocks (NIB's), talk to your *m*BIT Coach and get them to help you dissolve and pattern-interrupt those NIB's and then return to Step 4 above and re-do the steps of the exercise till you can experience deep integrated satiation of any compulsive feelings.

Notes/Thoughts/Insights:

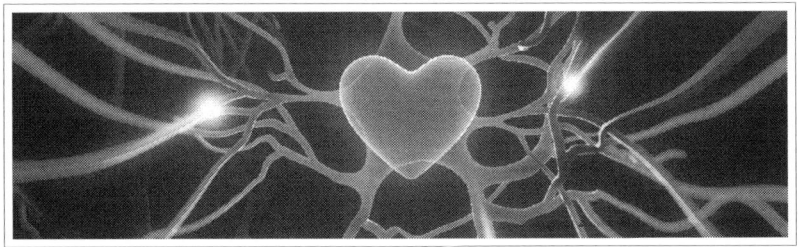

16.

Wisdom, Emergence and Personal Evolution

"Knowledge comes from but a single perspective; wisdom comes from multiple perspectives."

Gregory Bateson

According to Gregory Bateson, the great anthropologist, philosopher and systems theorist, wisdom requires multiple perspectives. In his typically thought-provoking style, Bateson was known to say "there is no inherent wisdom in only one point of reference." So wisdom requires the intelligence and intuition of all of your brains aligned together.

Wisdom also involves action and expression into the world. Wisdom that is not embodied in pragmatic action is not wisdom at all, it's merely entertaining ideas. What's more, ideas that don't guide or generate change in the world are a waste of valuable time and effort. They're more like puerile fantasies than wise ideas.

And out of wisdom and aligned action, comes personal evolution. It's about inspiring the human spirit, inspiring your self to evolve and transform your world in generative and wise ways. You can make a difference, to yourself, those you love and care for and to your world. And with neuro-genesis – the neural plasticity to evolve and change the very neural structures of your brain – you can literally evolve your consciousness and your capacity for thinking, feeling and *'being'* in new ways. So with this exercise, deeply enjoy exploring the various aspects of possibility in bringing wisdom, emergence and personal evolution to your mind and life.

Wisdom through the Prime Functions of each Brain

 What would be a wiser set of values for your life that would encourage you to flourish and come fully alive? What values inspire you?

What would be wiser ways of feeling that would support you to come alive and live and act more fully?

What would be wiser ways of connecting with both yourself and others that would allow you to truly live to your highest sense of self?

What would be wiser ways of thinking and making meaning that would allow you to really come alive and open your mind to new and creative possibilities?

What would be wiser ways of perceiving that would help you experience your world in more generative ways?

What would be wiser ways of deeply experiencing your core-self that would allow you to live more fully?

What would be wiser ways of acting and moving in the world that would deeply support you to make the most of your life?

What would be wiser ways of self-preservation and setting boundaries, of responding to perceived threats, and ways of doing gutsy courage, that would allow you to generate a life you deeply and truly need to live to express your highest self?

Looking at what you written above, what ideas come up for you about what would be a wiser and more generative way to truly evolve your self and your world? What would make a difference to your world? How can you live so that you are living a wiser and more compelling life?

Bringing your Human Spirit alive - flourishing and evolving

 What makes your heart sing and come alive? What passions and dreams bring your spirit alive? What are your compassionate and inspiring hopes, personal visions and aspirations you hold in your heart for your life?

What makes your brain light up? What creative ideas and thoughts capture your attention and bring your mind fully alive?

What moves you deeply? What makes your gut fill with drive, motivation and courageous action? What makes your deepest sense of the courageous you come fully alive?

Describe your *'ideal self'* – the higher expression of your self. What is your best and most inspiring self like? Ask yourself: What is my ideal life and work? What will I be doing? What will I be creating? What will I be feeling? Where will I be? Who will I be with? What sort of person will I be? What contribution will I be making? How will I be living? How will I be evolving? Explore this in relation to your own self, your intimate and significant relationships, your family, your work and career, your wealth creating, your community, your place in the Universe.

Looking at what you've written above, what ideas come up for you about what would be a way of being, a way of action, a way of living that will truly bring your human spirit alive, that will allow you to flourish and to live a life of true meaning and deep purpose and that will be a wiser way of living?

Generative Learning: Future Pacing the next *m*BIT Coaching Session

Reflections and Learnings

Points to discuss at the next session

Coaching outcomes I'd like to pursue/explore

Acknowledgements

We would like to thank and acknowledge all the people who made this publication possible.

A big thank you to all the *m*BIT Trainers and *m*BIT Coaches who undertook action research testing and trialing of the exercises in this Workbook, and all those kind and generous Clients who piloted the exercises in their *m*BIT Coaching sessions. And in particular a special thank you to Fiona Soosalu, Dr. Suzanne Henwood, David McCombe and Pauline Wong for their brilliant feedback, advice and suggestions. Without everyone's wonderful support, connection and interest this *m*BIT Coaching Workbook wouldn't be as grounded and integrated as you all helped us make it.

We'd also like to thank the following authors and researchers for their very kind permission to quote or reference their excellent work: Prof. Eugene Gendlin, Gavin de Becker, Joy Ainley, Stephen Elliot, The Institute of HeartMath, Mantak Chia, Will Scully, Mary O'Malley and Ken Marslew. And we'd also like to acknowledge that Coherent Breathing® is a registered trademark of Coherence LLC and that HeartMath® is a registered trademark of the Institute of HeartMath.

We'd really like to share our appreciation and special thanks to Sebastian Kaulitzki of SciePro.com and Alyssa and Murray Finlay of Artifact Design Group for all their fantastic art and graphics design work.

Lastly and most importantly, from deep in our hearts we'd like to thank the beautiful and wonderful ladies in our lives. Fiona, Cherie, Karis and Sachi, your love, support and encouragement continue to fill our lives with magic. Thank you.

Legal stuff

As indicated at the front of this publication, the authors and publisher have used their best efforts in preparing this book. This publication contains exercises, ideas, opinions, tips and techniques for improving wisdom and human performance. The materials are intended to provide helpful and useful material on the subjects addressed in the publication. The publisher and authors do *not* provide or purport to provide you with any medical, health, psychological or professional advice or service or any other personal professional service. You should seek the advice of your own medical practitioner, health professional or other relevant competent professional before trying or using information, exercises or techniques described in this publication. In addition, you should always utilize the services of a trained certified *m*BIT Coach when using this Workbook or when undertaking the exercises within it, and do so under the *m*BIT Coach's guidance.

The publisher and authors, jointly and severally, make no representations or warranties with respect to the accuracy, reliability, sufficiency or completeness of the contents of this publication and specifically disclaim any implied warranties or merchantability or fitness for any particular purpose. There are no warranties which extend beyond the descriptions contained in this paragraph. The accuracy and completeness of the information provided herein and the opinions stated herein are not guarantees, nor warranties to or towards the production of any particular result, and the advice and strategies contained herein may not be suitable for every individual.

You read and use this publication with the explicit understanding that neither the publisher, nor authors shall be liable for any direct or indirect loss of profit or any other commercial damages, including but not limited to special, incidental, punitive, consequential or other damages. In reading or using any part or portion of this publication, you agree to not hold, nor attempt to hold the publisher or authors liable for any loss, liability, claim, demand, damage and all legal cost or other expenses arising whatsoever in connection with the use, misuse or inability to use the materials. In jurisdictions that exclude such limitations, liability is limited to the consideration paid by you for the right to view or use these materials, and/or the greatest extent permitted by law.

About the authors

Grant Soosalu

Grant Soosalu is the co-developer of the growing field of *m*BIT (multiple Brain Integration Techniques). *m*BIT is being hailed as a ground-breaking synthesis of the latest research in neurology and cognitive science, and a true advancement of the field of NLP.

Grant is a highly sought after international Trainer, Leadership Consultant and Executive Coach with extensive backgrounds in Organisational Change, Training and Leadership Development. He has advanced degrees and certifications in Applied Physics, Psychology, Positive Psychology, Computer Engineering and System Development. He is also a qualified Total Quality Management (TQM) Trainer, and has achieved Master Practitioner Certification in the behavioral sciences of NLP and Advanced Behavioral Modeling. More recently Grant was awarded a Graduate Coaching Diploma in the newly emerging field of Authentic Happiness Coaching.

Grant has wide ranging expertise and extensive experience in the educational sector as a Senior Lecturer, Coach, Training Developer and Facilitator. He also has extensive backgrounds in Behavioral Modeling, Business Development, Senior Technical Consulting and Project and Change Management. Grant provides coaching and mentoring to numerous CEO's and Senior Executives.

Currently, Grant is a Consultant Lecturer at a leading Australian University where he runs workshops and programs on Social Media Marketing and the applications of Positive Psychology to Conflict Resolution, Risk Management and Organizational Change. Grant also runs a successful consulting company providing services to organizations predominantly in the finance sector.

Grant has published articles and papers in International Journals, in the fields of Training, Leadership, Applied Physics, Philosophy and Neuro Linguistic Programming.

Marvin Oka

Marvin is a co-developer of the field of *m*BIT and a highly sought after international consultant and speaker specializing in leading edge behavioral change technologies and research. Recognized as a world leader and authority in his field, Marvin has built an impressive track record helping organizations with strategic, systemic and cultural change. Marvin's clients range from private enterprises to government agencies throughout the world.

Marvin's professional background is in the innovative and groundbreaking field of Behavioral Modeling. This exciting field examines various forms of human talent, ability and expertise, and then seeks to create models and methods to replicate these forms of superior performance in others. Marvin is one of only five people in the world who have been recognized by his peers with the rare title of *'Certified Master Behavioral Modeler'*. Additionally Marvin was one of the first five people to achieve the accredited status of a *'Certified NLP Master Trainer'* in the field of Neuro Linguistic Programming (NLP), and at that time was the youngest ever to have reached this level of professional competency.

Born in Honolulu, Hawaii and now living in Australia, Marvin is one of the founding Directors and is on the board of the International NLP Trainers Association (INLPTA) based in Washington, DC, with representation in over 42 countries worldwide.

References and resources

Extensive references, bibliography, suggested readings and additional resources for the work described in this publication can be found at:

www.mbraining.com

and

http://enhancingmylife.blogspot.com

Made in the USA
Charleston, SC
11 March 2014